Republic of North Macedonia.

The History and A Guide to Tourism

Author
David Thompson

Copyright Policy

Information-Source This Title is protected by Copyright Policy, any intention to reproduce, distribute and sales of this Title without the permission from the Title owner is strictly prohibited. Please when purchasing this Title, make sure that you obtain the necessary reference related to the purchase such as purchasing receipt. In accordance with this term, you are permitted to have access to this Title. Thanks for understanding and cooperation.

All-right reserved Information-Sourve
Copyright 2021..

Published
By
Information-Source.
16192 Coastal Highway Lewes,
DE 19958. USA.

Table of Content

NORTH MACEDONIA 1
- INTRODUCTION 1
- LAND 3
  - Relief 3
  - Drainage 4
  - Climate 4
  - Plant and animal life 4
- PEOPLE OF NORTH MACEDONIA 5
  - Ethnic groups 11
  - Language 12
  - Religion 12
  - Settlement patterns 12
  - Demographic trends 13
  - Traditional Costumes of Macedonia 13
- ECONOMY 16
  - Agriculture of North Macedonia 18
  - Resources and power 18
  - Manufacturing 18
  - Finance 18
  - Trade 19
  - Transportation and communications 19
- GOVERNMENT AND SOCIETY 19
  - Constitutional framework 19
  - Local government and Justice 20
  - Political process 20
  - Security, Health and welfare 21
  - Education 22
- CULTURAL LIFE 22
  - Daily life and social customs 27
  - The arts 28
  - Cultural institutions 28
  - Sports and recreation 29
  - Media and publishing 29
- GASTRONOMY OF MACEDONIA 30
- HISTORY OF NORTH MACEDONIA 35
  - The ancient world 35
  - The medieval states 37
  - The Ottoman Empire 38

The independence movement 40
War and partition 41
The republic 42
Independence of North Macedonia 44
INFORMATION TOURISM, SITES AND LANDMARKS 53
Bargala Archaeological Site 61
Bitola 62
Dojran Lake 66
Galičica National Park 69
Heraclea Lyncestis Archaeological Site 70
Jakupica Mountain 71
Kokino Megalithic Observatory 72
Korab Mountain 74
Kratovo 75
Krushevo Kruševo 81
Kumanovo Zebrnjak Memorial 85
Lesnovo Monastery 92
Mariovo Morihovo 97
Marko's Monastery Susica 101
Matejce Monastery 103
Matka Canyon 107
Mavrovo National Park 113
Nidze Mountain Kajmakchalan 118
Ohrid 121
Osogovo Mountains 127
Pelister National Park 128
Prespa Lake Prespa Region 131
Prilep 136
Radika River 145
Saint Archangel Michael Monastery Štip 147
Holy Archangel Michael Monastery Varos 149
Saint George Monastery Kurbinovo village 151
Saint Joachim Monastery Osogovo 153
Saint George Monastery Staro Nagoričane village 155
Saint Joachim Monastery Osogovo 159
Saint John Bigorski Monastery 161
Saint Nicholas Monastery Psaca 166
Saint Panteleimon Monastery Nerezi village 169
Sar planina Mountain Sharr Mountain 172
Skopje 176
Scupi Archaeological Site 182

Stobi Archaeological Site 184
Struga 186
Trebeništa Trebenishte 187
Treskavec Monastery 188
Veles 190
Veljuša Monastery 195
Vevčani Village Vevcani Springs 197
Vodoca Monastery 199
Zrze Monastery Zrze village 201

North Macedonia
Introduction

North Macedonia, country of the south-central Balkans. It is bordered to the north by Kosovo and Serbia, to the east by Bulgaria, to the south by Greece, and to the west by Albania. The capital is Skopje.

The Republic of North Macedonia is located in the northern part of the area traditionally known as Macedonia, a geographical region bounded to the south by the Aegean Sea and the Aliákmon River; to the west by Lakes Prespa and Ohrid, the watershed west of the Crni Drim River, and the Šar Mountains; and to the north by the mountains of the Skopska Crna Gora and the watershed between the Morava and Vardar river basins. The Pirin Mountains mark its eastern edge. The Republic of North Macedonia occupies about two-fifths of the entire geographical region of Macedonia. The rest of the region belongs to Greece and Bulgaria. Most people with a Macedonian identity also refer to the region that constitutes North Macedonia as Vardar Macedonia, the Greek part of Macedonia as Aegean Macedonia, and the Bulgarian part of Macedonia as Pirin Macedonia. In this article, unless otherwise indicated, the name Macedonia refers to the present-day state of the Republic of North Macedonia when discussing geography and history since 1913 and to the larger region as described above when used in earlier historical contexts.

The region of Macedonia owes its importance neither to its size nor to its population but rather to its location at a major junction of communication routes in particular, the great north-south route from the Danube River to the Aegean formed by the valleys of the Morava and Vardar rivers and the ancient east-west trade routes connecting the Black Sea and Istanbul with the Adriatic Sea. Although the majority of the republic's inhabitants are of Slavic descent and heirs to the Eastern Orthodox tradition of Christianity, 500 years of incorporation into the Ottoman Empire left substantial numbers of other ethnic groups, including Albanians, Turks, Vlachs (Aromani), and Roma (Gypsies). Consequently, Macedonia forms a complex border zone between the major cultural traditions of Europe and Asia.

Ottoman control was brought to an end by the Balkan Wars (1912–13), after which Macedonia was divided among Greece, Bulgaria, and Serbia. Following World War I, the Serbian segment was incorporated into the Kingdom of Serbs, Croats, and Slovenes (renamed Yugoslavia in 1929). After World War II the Serbian part of Macedonia became a constituent republic within the Federal People's Republic of Yugoslavia (later Socialist Federal Republic of Yugoslavia). The collapse of Yugoslavia led the Republic of Macedonia to declare its independence on September 17, 1991.

The two major problems facing the newly independent Republic of Macedonia were ensuring for its large Albanian minority the rights of full citizenship and gaining international recognition under its constitutional name and membership in international organizations in the face of strong opposition from Greece, which claimed a monopoly on the use of the term Macedonia. (See Researcher's Note: Macedonia: a contested name.) After years of largely fruitless UN-mediated negotiations regarding the name issue, in June 2018 Macedonian Prime Minister Zoran Zaev and Greek Prime Minister Alexis Tsipras announced that an agreement (thereafter known as the Prespa Agreement) had been reached under which the Macedonian republic would be known both domestically and internationally as the Republic of North Macedonia (Macedonian: Severna Makedonija). By January 2019 the Macedonian and Greek legislatures had both approved the measures necessary to pave the way for formal adoption of the new name, which came into effect on February 12, 2019.

Land

Relief

Geologically, North Macedonia consists mainly of heavily folded ancient metamorphic rocks, which in the west have been eroded to reveal older granites. In the central region are found sedimentary deposits of more recent age. Traversing the country from north to south is a series of active fault lines, along which earthquakes frequently occur. The most severe of these in recent history occurred at Debar in 1967. Skopje was largely destroyed by an earthquake in 1963.

The mobility of Earth's crust has also created two tectonic lakes, Prespa and Ohrid, in the southwest and has resulted in the formation of several mineral springs and hot springs.

North Macedonia is largely mountainous, with many peaks rising above the tree line at 6,600 feet (2,000 metres) above sea level. The highest elevation is at Mount Korab (9,030 feet, or 2,752 metres) on the Albanian border. Near the Šar Mountains in the northwest, the country is covered with forest. Where this has been cleared (and often in the past overgrazed), the thin skeletal soils have been subjected to dramatic erosion and gullying. There are also several broad and fertile valleys that provide good potential for agriculture.

Drainage

The greater part of North Macedonia (about nine-tenths of its area) drains southeastward into the Aegean Sea via the Vardar River and its tributaries. Smaller parts of this basin drain into Lake Doiran (Macedonian: Dojran) and into the Aegean via the Strumica and Struma rivers. The remainder of North Macedonia drains northward via the Crni Drim River toward the Adriatic Sea.

The convoluted and fractured geology of the area imposes upon many of these rivers erratic courses that frequently drive through narrow and sometimes spectacular gorges. Such formations facilitate the damming of rivers for electric power generation.

Climate

North Macedonia stands at the junction of two main climatic zones, the Mediterranean and the continental. Periodically, air breaks through mountain barriers to the north and south, bringing dramatically contrasting weather patterns; one example is the cold northerly wind known as the vardarec. Overall, there is a moderate continental climate: temperatures average in the low 30s F (about 0 °C) in January and rise to the high 60s and 70s F (about 20–25 °C) in July. Annual precipitation is relatively light, between about 20 and 28 inches (about 500 and 700 mm). Rainfalls of less than 1 inch (25.4 mm) in the driest months (July–August) rise to nearly 4 inches (about 100 mm) in October–November. Because of differences in local aspect and relief, there may be considerable variation in the climate, the eastern areas tending to have milder winters and hotter, drier summers and the western (more mountainous) regions having more severe winters.

Plant and animal life

The mountainous northwestern parts of North Macedonia support large areas of forest vegetation. On the lower slopes this is principally deciduous woodland, but conifers grow at elevations as high as 6,600 feet (2,000 metres). Some areas of forest have been cleared to provide rough summer pasture. The forests support a variety of wildlife, including wild pigs, wolves, bears, and lynx. The dry and warm summers result in an abundance of insect life, with species of grasshoppers much in evidence, along with numerous small lizards.

People of North Macedonia

Macedonians are outstandingly warm, cheerful, open, hospitable, simple, *friendly and lovely people*, whose innate features and cordial attitude you immediately spot the very moment you meet them. *You instantly learn that Macedonians love their country by the way they inoffensively greet you and show you around.*

The Macedonians are the southern Slavic people of the Illyrian-Thracian origin who speak the Macedonian language which is a part of the South Slavic group of languages. Structurally, Macedonian language is closest to Serbian and Bulgarian than any other Slavonic language. The current form of the Macedonian language has accumulated a thriving Slavic literary tradition and was codified after the Second World War. The Macedonian language is in the same family as Russian, Serbian or Bulgarian, but is distinctly different. The official alphabet in Macedonia is the *Cyrillic*, but Latin is used also.

Macedonia has been continuously settled since prehistory. The modern Macedonians developed as a result of the mixing of the Slavs that came on the Balkans in 6th AD century, with local peoples that were living in the Macedonia prior to their coming. By absorbing the peoples living in Macedonia, the Slavs also absorbed their culture, and in that amalgamation a people was gradually formed with predominantly Slavic ethnic elements, speaking a

Slavic language and with a Slavic-Byzantine culture. In 581 AD, on the territory of Macedonia, the Slavs created their own country-like formation called the *Macedonian Sclavinia,* which waged several wars against the Byzantium Empire. In 686 AD, the last Macedonian Sclavinia was occupied by the Byzantium and the Bulgarians. In mid 8th century, the Macedonian Slavs under Byzantine rule were baptized and accepted Christianity, and the Macedonians under Bulgarian rule became Christians in the 9th century. When Samuel founded his Macedonian Empire in 976 Bulgaria was already conquered by Byzantium /971/.

The Macedonians have a great role in the creation of the Slavic writing. The local dialect of the Macedonian Slavs spoken north of Thessaloniki became the basis for Old Church Slavonic, the first literary Slavic language. During the whole medieval period, Macedonia was constantly an object of conquest and was being slipped from Byzantine, to Bulgaria, to Serbia. This ended in the 14th century when Macedonia, together with the whole Balkan region was conquered by the Ottoman Turks. After the creation of the Greek, Bulgarian and Serbian states who gained independence from Turkey, the three young countries started opening Greek, Bulgarian and Serbian churches and propagandist schools, in order to assimilate the Macedonian population through education. The rivalry succeeded in dividing the Macedonians into three distinct parties, the pro-Bulgarian /which was the largest/, pro-Greek and pro-Serbian one, at the expense of development of a unique Macedonian identity.

In the middle of the 15th century the krajina vilayets of Roumelia in Macedonia were : Skopje, Kalkandelen /Tetovo/, Gornji i Donji Debar, Dugo Brdo, Reka, Čemernica, Veles, Prilep, Bitolj, Kičevo and other on the territories of Kosovo, Raška and Bosnia with vilayets of : Pastric later Paštrik, Vlk the area ruled by Vuk Branković, Priština,

Zvečan, Jeleč, Ras, Sjenica, Nikšići Vlasi-Wallachians of Nikšić and Hodidjed Saray-ovasi.

The *Old Serbia and Macedonia i.e. the South Serbia* in the narrow sense considers those areas that were liberated after the Balkan wars from the five centuries long Turkish yoke, and by the Bucharest Peace Treaty in 1913 united with the Kingdom of Serbia and Montenegro. Those are areas in the valleys of the Lim, Ibar and Raska Rivers, Metohija, Kosovo and Vardar Macedonia the Skopje basin, Kumanovo-Preševo Valley, area by the Pcinja and Kriva rivers, Kocani Valley, Maleš-Osogovo Mountains, Plauš and Strumica, Veleš Valley, basins of the Topolka and Babuna, Has and Klepci areas, Rajac and Tikveš, Morihovo, Meglen, Tziga Valley, Đevđelija Valley, Bojmija, Demir Kapija Železnik, Solunska kampanja i zaliv Thessaloniki and Bay, Pajak, Thessaloniki, Drama, Dojran and Seres Valleys, Trakia, basin of the Marica River, Ajvasilsko and Bešič lakes, Dojran Lake, Epirus and South Albania, West Macedonia, Poreč, Kičevo, Kopač, Kačanik Gorge, Tetovo Valley, Suhodolica, Šar planina Mountain, Kosovo, Metohija, Prizren area, Rogozna Mountain, Novi Pazar area, Šekular, Plav and Gusinje.

The issue of the future destiny of Stara Srbija Old Serbia and Macedonia, that included the Ottoman vilayets of Kosovo, Bitolj and Thessaloniki was one of the main open and disagreement questions of the European diplomacy in the last decades of the 19th and the beginning of the 20th century. The neighboring Balkan states of Serbia, Bulgaria and Greece, but also the great powers were interested for the so-called '*Macedonian question*' as the fate of the Turkish European provinces.

At the Salonica front also known as Macedonia front /which was military theater in 1916 in attempt by the Allies to help Serbia against the combined attack of Germany, Austria-Hungary and Bulgaria/, there was a Russian brigade sent by the Tsar Nikolai to aid the Serbian Army as the Russian Empire was a major supporter of Serbia. The English were extremely upset about this event and they did everything to isolate the Russian brigade which the British generals considered the great threat to their interests. They successfully made the Russian brigade transferred from the Salonica front. This Russian brigade was sent far to the east of Greece to avoid any contact with the Serbian Army. Just then the British enmity toward Serbia was expressed in the most cruel way, as they started with the most despicable blackmails. In the hardest moment, Serbia asked for the financial aid of 800 thousands of pounds sterling as the loan for renewal of armament, and medicaments and sanitary equipment. The Brits responded with blackmail you Serbs will get the loan under the condition to renounce your territory in east of Macedonia in favor of Bulgaria. This ultimatum was firmly rejected by Serbia.

In the period between 1903 and 1908 the three Balkan countries started arming the three different parties and stimulating them to fight one another. This period of the history of Macedonia is called the Macedonian Struggle, and is manifested with brother killing his own brother for being a partisan of the different nationalist propaganda. This period lasted till 1912, when Macedonia was divided between Greece, Bulgaria and Serbia. In those dark days the National Awakening of the Macedonians took place. In late 19th and early 20th century several Macedonian intellectuals living abroad propagated the idea of the unique character of the Macedonians, that is, that the Slavic-speakers of Macedonia compose a separate ethnicity which is different from Serbian, Bulgarian and Greek. After the Balkan Wars, following division of the region of Macedonia among the Kingdom of Greece, the Kingdom of Bulgaria and the Kingdom of Serbia, and after WWI, during which Macedonia was ruled by Bulgaria /1914-1918/ in return for supporting Axis, the idea of belonging to a separate

Macedonian nation was further spread among the Macedonians. The suffering during the wars, the endless struggle of the Balkan monarchies on dominance over the population made the Macedonians more and more aware that the creation of an independent Macedonian state and a development of a Macedonian nation would put an end of their suffering. The first revolutionary organization that promoted the existence of a separate ethnic Macedonian nation was United IMRO created in 1925 and composed of Macedonians with leftist ideology. This idea was internationalized and backed by the Comintern which issued in 1934 a declaration supporting the further development of the Macedonian nation. This action was backed by the Bulgarian, Greek and Yugoslav communist parties and they started supporting the national consolidation of the Macedonian people and created Macedonian sections within the parties, headed by a prominent IMRO (United) member.

From a demographic standpoint, the population was slowly increasing prior to World War II, and has been increasing more rapidly since then. A substantial migration from villages to towns has been occurring over the last 60 years. In World War II, Macedonia was occupied by Italian, German and Bulgarian troops. Macedonia was annexed and divided between Greater Albania and Greater Bulgaria following the invasion and occupation of Yugoslavia in April, 1941 by Germany and Axis allies Italy, Hungary, Albania and Bulgaria. The Tetovo, Gostivar, Struga, Kicevo and Debar districts of Western Macedonia were annexed and incorporated into an enlarged Albanian state, of Greater Albania, sponsored by Adolf Hitler and Benito Mussolini. Western Macedonia was occupied by the Italian army and was under Italian administration until the Italian surrender in 1943 when it was re-occupied by Germany. In conjunction with the Balli Kombetar, the Italian occupation forces formed the fascist Albanian Ljuboten battalion which the German forces retained after 1943. In 1944, Germany formed the Albanian Skanderber Waffen SS Division which occupied Kosovo, Southern Serbia, Montenegro and Western Macedonia. The Macedonian Orthodox, Serbian Orthodox, Roma and Macedonian Jewish population were the targets of victims of genocide and extermination. The Macedonian and Serbian nationalities were de-recognized by the Bulgarian occupation forces. The Bulgarian occupation regime categorized the Macedonian Slav population as Bulgarian. In the Greater Albania of Western Macedonia, the Macedonian Orthodox, Serbian Orthodox, Roma and Jewish population were similarly targeted for elimination and deportation. read more Carl K. Savich Holocaus in Macedonia, 1941-1944.

In mid 1941 the first Macedonian partisan units were created, and organized attacks on targets in the cities of Kumanovo and Prilep, as the Macedonian people took part in the Second World War side by side with the Allied forces, with the other people of Yugoslavia. The first greater partisan battalion was formed in 1943, and the same year the armed struggle against the fascist occupation was conducted in every part of Macedonia. On August 2, 1944 the ASNOM (Anti-Fascist Assembly of the National Liberation of Macedonia) was held on which the decisions were made for the establishment of the Macedonian State, as a federal unit within the framework of the Yugoslav federation, and the officiousness of the Macedonian language. During the period September November 1944 the Macedonian Partisan Army has taken the final offensives which resulted in the liberation of the whole of the territory of Vardar Macedonia.

After being nearly 50 years the federal republic of Yugoslavia, on 8 September 1991 Macedonia proclaimed its independence. Over the period since achieving its independence, the Republic of Macedonia has been striving to build a stable political and economic community, with a legal system able to facilitate rapid integration into the European Union and the wider international community. From 1991 till today the Republic of Macedonia has been walking the road towards integration in the Euro-Atlantic structures. Since the early 1990s, many Macedonians embraced the view that their identity stems from 2,500 years ago in antiquity, while many Macedonians also feel very proud of their Slav origin.

Macedonians are the warmest people in the Balkans and keen to make their guests feel at home, starting with their tasty food, to love for music and dance and overall merrymaking... If Kosovo is heart of Serbia, than Macedonia is soul of Serbia.

Ethnic groups

The population of the Republic of North Macedonia is diverse. At the beginning of the 21st century, nearly two-thirds of the population identified themselves as Macedonians. Macedonians generally trace their descent to the Slavic tribes that moved into the region between the 6th and 8th centuries CE. Albanians are the largest and most-important minority in the Republic of North Macedonia. According to the 2002 census, they made up about one-fourth of the population. The Albanians most of whom trace their descent to the ancient Illyrians are concentrated in the northwestern part of the country, near the borders with Albania and Kosovo. Albanians form majorities in some 16 of North Macedonia's 80 municipalities. Other, much smaller minorities (constituting less than 5 percent of the population each) include the Turks, Roma, Serbs, Bosniaks, and Vlachs (Aromani). The Turkish minority is mostly scattered across central and western North Macedonia, a legacy of the 500-year rule of the Ottoman Empire. The majority of Vlachs, who speak a language closely related to Romanian, live in the old mountain city of Kruševo.

Language

The Macedonian language is very closely related to Bulgarian and Serbo-Croatian and is written in the Cyrillic script. When Serbian rule replaced that of the Ottoman Turks in 1913, the Serbs officially denied Macedonian linguistic distinctness and treated the Macedonian language as a dialect of Serbo-Croatian. The Macedonian language was not officially recognized until the establishment of Macedonia as a constituent republic of communist Yugoslavia in 1945.

Religion

Religious affiliation is a particularly important subject in North Macedonia because it is so closely tied to ethnic and national identity. With the exception of Bosniaks, the majority of Slavic speakers living in the region of Macedonia are Orthodox Christian. Macedonians, Serbs, and Bulgarians, however, have established their own autocephalous Orthodox churches in an effort to assert the legitimacy of their national identities. The majority Greeks in the region of Greek Macedonia, who also identify themselves as Macedonians, are Orthodox as well, but they belong to the Greek Orthodox Church. Turks and the great majority of both Albanians and Roma are Muslims. Altogether, about one-third of the population is of the Islamic faith.

Settlement patterns

Successive waves of migration, as well as economic and political modernization, have left their mark in a diversity of settlement patterns. The inhabitants of the highlands are generally shepherds. In more fertile areas, small-scale subsistence and market-oriented agriculture are practiced. Several small market towns are of great antiquity. In Roman times Bitola was a commercial centre known as Heraclea Lyncestis. Ohrid became a major administrative and ecclesiastical centre in the early Middle Ages. The coming of the Ottoman Turks in the 14th century promoted the growth of Skopje as a governmental and military centre and created large agrarian estates, which were later socialized by the communists and given over to extensive mechanized cultivation. This latter process was responsible for the growth, beginning in 1945, of Kavardarci and Veles.

Industrialization in the second half of the 20th century had a dramatic impact upon population distribution. The population of Skopje grew to nearly one-fourth of the population of the republic, its attractiveness as a pole for migration having been enhanced both by its location at a transcontinental transportation route and by its status as the republic's capital. Acting as a reasonably effective counterforce to the pull of Skopje is the growth of tourism around Ohrid. At the beginning of the 21st century, about three-fifths of the population of North Macedonia was urban.

Demographic trends

Historically, the Balkans have experienced high rates of natural increase in population. The rate declined remarkably in the 20th century in response to industrialization and urbanization. The rate of natural increase in North Macedonia at the end of the first decade of the 21st century was about three-fifths less than it had been in the mid-1990s. Birth rates for the same period declined relatively steadily by about one-fifth, to about three-fifths of the world average. Movement from rural to urban areas in North Macedonia in the early 21st century was much more common than the reverse. Emigration to other parts of Europe, as well as to North America and Australia, has also had a significant influence on demographic trends in North Macedonia.

Traditional Costumes of Macedonia

There are around 70 various types of richly decorated traditional costumes in Macedonia. Macedonian traditional costumes are divided into two main types : west Macedonian and east Macedonian traditional costumes. According to the ethnographic zones, the western Macedonian traditional costumes come as the Upper course of Vardar River zone, the Debar-Mijak and the Brsjak zones, while the east Macedonian traditional costumes are divided as the Middle course of the Vardar River zone and the Shopi region.

Prilep Valley National Dress *traditional costume of Mariovo* the Prilep region is found in most of the settlements of the Prilep valley, i.e. in the north-east part of the Pelagonia plain. Prilep Valley traditional costume is similar to the dress in the Bitola valley and forms a complete whole with it, except for certain minor differences in the nuances of color and the embroidery technique. In the Prilep valley dress flame red and blood yellow are the dominant colors, while in the Bitola valley dress the dominant colors are blood yellow and black. The traditional costume of the Mariovo area (Prilep valley area) is one of the most decorative and richly ornamented, especially abounding in metal and bead ornaments. A slight Byzantine influence makes itself felt via the old "bolyar" costume, particularly in the manner of veiling and the decoration of the clothes. This costume is one of the most over elaborate in Macedonia, especially the bridal dress. The brides wear: golema /large/ smock, almost entirely covered with embroidery on the sleeves (the decorations used are "vrteshkki" circles). The fronts and the "okolizhot" the border round the skirt, are embroidered with "shapkite" formalized blossoms and "kopito poli" horseshoes, knitted of multi-colored woolen thread and worn on the arms below the elbow cuffs, upper garment of broadcloth called "valanka" ornamented with embroidered facings with gold and yellow thread. The seams are trimmed with tufted fringe and braid, girdle plaited from black wool, an apron which is a special part of the bridal dress, folk-weave, patterned with "kolci" (rhomboids), "krshchinja" (crosses), and trimmed at the hemline with red tufted fringe, gold thread ribbon, and braid, an ornament worn below the girdle at the back made of beads and trimmed with old silver coins, metal ornaments for the belt which is the Silversmith's work, a silver ornament to go under the belt, trimmed with old silver coins with seven rows of chains, "uskolec", a bead-work ornament worn at the sides of the belt, necklace in the form of a stomacher, trimmed with old silver coins, mounted with broadcloth, flame colored socks knitted and patterned with formalized blossoms, fes a head dress with rows of old silver coins "tunturici", which hang down the sides of the face. The silver boss is ornamented with various colored stones and trimmed with pendants. Above the *fes* there is a garland of spruce, white broadcloth towel decorated with embroidery and two rows of old coins and a hair decoration made from black twisted woolen fringe which is worn hanging down the shoulders......

The men in Mariovo region wore the following: *"rubina"* smock or shirt, a girdle, *"sukman"* a kind of upper garment, *"chakshiri"* breeches and gaiters which have been retained till now in the man's dress from Mariovo, a coat with sleeves which was worn either as a shirt or on top of the jacket. Each of these features has been preserved in the contemporary national dress traditional costume of Macedonia.

Tanec Professional Folklore Ensemble Macedonia

Tanec is eminent professional folklore musical ensemble from Skopje, Republic of Macedonia, and one of the most famous and reputed folklore ensembles in the Balkans. Tanec Ensemble is worldwide considered as an ambassador of the Macedonian folklore tradition, with the repertoire that includes more than 60 choreographed pieces. The Tanec Ensemble of folklore dances and songs of Macedonia was founded by the Government of the People's Republic of Macedonia in 1949 with an aim to collect, preserve and present the Macedonian folklore: *folk songs and folk dances*, folk instruments, national costumes etc. The Tanec Ensemble Macedonia inspired by ancient Macedonian culture and traditions also has a junior ensemble. During the several decades of its existence the Tanec Ensemble has taken part in over 3500 concerts and festivals around the world including: USA, Canada, Australia, Japan, USSR, France, Belgium, Germany, Switzerland, Italy, Greece, Turkey, Kuwait, Israel, Egypt, Nigeria, Mali, Senegal, Zaire and many other countries as well as concerts across the former Socialist Federal Republic of Yugoslavia….The highly professional performances of "Tanec", proven on the world's most renowned stages, make the ensemble most competent researcher and performer of the music folklore of the Republic of Macedonia, as evidenced by over eight million spectators and numerous awards that "Tanec" received for its achievements in the preservation and nurturing of the Macedonian folklore and the years-long presentation of the artistic values of the traditional folk dances and songs at home and abroad, thus making a remarkable contribution to the affirmation of the Macedonian cultural legacy.

Economy

Along with the rest of the Balkan Peninsula, Macedonia underwent an impressive economic transformation after 1945 in this case within the framework provided by Yugoslavia's system of "socialist self-management." Even so, Macedonia remained the poorest of the Yugoslav republics and was included throughout the communist period in the list of regions that merited economic aid from wealthier parts of the federation. While this status undoubtedly brought much investment, several projects were placed without adequate attention to the supply of materials or access to markets.

A prime example was the choice of Skopje as the site for a steel industry.

Although socialized production dominated industrial and commercial life after the communists' rise to power in 1945, the private sector remained important in agriculture, craft production, and retail trade. About 70 percent of agricultural land was held privately, accounting for some 50 percent of output. However, privately owned enterprises were typically traditionalist in structure and outlook, and, even after the liberalization of the communist system in 1991, they were unable to develop a dynamic economic role.

Following the onset of the Yugoslav civil war in 1991, the economic position of Macedonia became very precarious. The republic had previously depended heavily on Yugoslav rather than foreign markets, and its participation in Yugoslavia's export trade was heavily skewed toward the countries of the former Soviet bloc, which were concurrently undergoing economic crises. United Nations sanctions against the rump Yugoslavia (the federation of Serbia and Montenegro) added to these difficulties by throttling the transport of goods through Macedonia. Also, an acrimonious dispute with Greece over the name of the republic frustrated Macedonia's quest for international recognition, thereby deterring foreign investment and delaying economic reform. By 2018 that dispute was resolved, with Macedonia officially becoming the Republic of North Macedonia.

As early as the mid-1990s, however, Macedonia had begun to find new trading partners, and the economy began to prosper. Though gross domestic product (GDP) dipped at the turn of the 21st century, it rebounded quickly, and the country weathered the worldwide economic downturn that began in 2008 better than many other countries. Nevertheless, unemployment remained high, exceeding 30 percent for much of the first decade of the 21st century.

Agriculture of North Macedonia

In the early 21st century the agricultural sector contributed about one-tenth of North Macedonia's GDP and engaged about one-sixth of the country's workforce. The main crops are tobacco, fruits (including apples and grapes), vegetables, wheat, rice, and corn (maize). Viticulture and dairy farming are also important.

Resources and power

Although there are deposits of zinc, iron, copper, lead, chromium, manganese, antimony, nickel, silver, and gold in North Macedonia, the country's mining industry is focused on the extraction of lignite (brown coal). More than three-fourths of North Macedonia's power is produced from fossil fuels (principally lignite). The remainder comes from hydroelectricity.

Manufacturing

Manufacturing constituted less than one-fifth of GDP in North Macedonia in the early 21st century and accounted for between one-tenth and one-fifth of employment. Because of the presence of mineral resources such as nickel, lead, and zinc in North Macedonia, ferrous and nonferrous metallurgy have long been linchpins of the country's manufacturing sector. Among the principal products associated with this industry are ferronickel, flat-rolled sheet steel, and seamed pipes. Automobile parts, electrical equipment, household appliances, and clothing are also produced, and there are wood- and plastic-processing industries

Finance

North Macedonia's national currency is the denar. The National Bank of the Republic of North Macedonia is the bank of issue, authorizes bank licensing, and oversees a system composed of banks (some of which are permitted to conduct only domestic business) and "savings houses." A large portion of capital in the banking system comes from foreign investors.

Trade

In the late 2010s North Macedonia's principal trading partners were Germany, Serbia, Greece, the United Kingdom, Bulgaria, Italy, and Romania. The country's main exports were iron and steel (especially ferronickel and flat-rolled products), clothing and accessories, and food products. Imports included machinery, petroleum, and iron and steel.

Transportation and communications

The location of the republic along the Morava-Vardar route from Belgrade, Serbia, to Thessaloníki, Greece, has endowed it with reasonably modern road and rail links on a northwest-southeast axis. North Macedonia's historic rail link with Greece passes through Bitola. The development of tourism in the Mavrovo-Ohrid area ensured new road building in the west. Airports at Skopje and Ohrid serve international destinations. By 2010 more than half of Macedonians had Internet access, a 35-fold increase in a period of just 10 years.

Government and society

Constitutional framework

The 1991 constitution of the newly independent republic established a republican assembly called the Sobranie consisting of a single chamber of 120 seats. There is an explicit separation of powers between the legislature, the judiciary, and the executive. The prime minister and cabinet ministers, for example, do not have seats in the assembly. The executive, under the prime minister, is the most powerful branch, with the legislature and judiciary acting principally as checks and balances to the government's activity. The president, who is elected to a five-year term, serves principally as a symbolic head of state and is the commander in chief of the armed forces; a president may serve no more than two terms. In 2001 the constitution was amended to include a number of provisions aimed at protecting the rights of the Albanian minority.

Local government and Justice

The republic is divided into 80 opštini (municipalities), to which are delegated many important social, judicial, and economic functions.

Justice

The legal system of North Macedonia is grounded in civil law. The judicial branch comprises basic and appellate courts, the Supreme Court, the Republican Judicial Council, and the Constitutional Court. The judges of the Constitutional Court are elected by the Sobranie.

Political process

All citizens age 18 and over are eligible to vote. Members of parliament are elected by popular vote on a proportional basis from party lists in six districts, each of which has 20 seats. During the era of federated Yugoslavia, the only authorized political party in Macedonia was the League of Communists of Macedonia. Since independence, dozens of parties have put forward electoral slates, and the elections of the early 21st century were dominated by a pair of large electoral coalitions. Headed by the Internal Macedonian Revolutionary Organization–Democratic Party for Macedonian National Unity (Vnatrešno-Makedonska Revolucionerna Organizacija–Demokratska Partija za Makedonsko

Nacionalno Edinstvo; VMRO-DPMNE), the Coalition for a Better Macedonia, which captured more than half of the seats in the parliamentary election of 2008, grew out of the National Unity coalition that had triumphed in the 2006 election. A number of smaller ethnic parties that joined the Coalition for a Better Macedonia previously had been members of the coalition led by the Social Democratic Union of Macedonia (Socijaldemosratski Sojuz na Makedonija; SDSM), the descendant of the League of Communists. That coalition, initially known as Together for Macedonia, evolved into the Sun Coalition for Europe, which captured nearly one-fourth of the seats in parliament in the 2008 election. Other significant political parties include the Democratic Union for Integration and the Democratic Party of Albanians. At the beginning of the 21st century, a concentrated effort was made to increase the involvement of women in politics and government, and the number of female representatives in the Sobranie grew from 8 in 2000 to 38 in 2011.

Security, Health and welfare

Military service in North Macedonia is voluntary. The principal component of the military is the army, augmented by the Air Wing, the Special Operations Regiment, and Logistic Support Command.

Health and welfare

The Ministry of Health oversees a compulsory state-funded health care system that requires employees and employers to pay contributions into the Health Insurance Fund. Private health care and private health insurance are also available. Among the top health priorities in North Macedonia identified by the Ministry of Health in the early 21st century were early detection and treatment of breast cancer, obligatory immunization, blood donation, prevention of tuberculosis and brucellosis, and HIV/AIDS prevention and treatment.

Education

Primary education is universal and compulsory for eight years from the age of seven. It may be conducted in languages other than Macedonian where there are large local majorities of other ethnic groups. A further four years of secondary education are available on a voluntary basis in specialized schools, which often represent the particular economic strengths or needs of a locality. Higher education is provided by colleges and pedagogical academies offering two-year courses, as well as by universities that offer two- to six-year courses in a range of disciplines. North Macedonia's universities include the South East European University in Tetovo, the University for Information Science and Technology "St. Paul the Apostle" in Ohrid, Saints Cyril and Methodius University in Skopje, the State University of Tetova, and "Goce Delcev" University in Stip.

Cultural life

The rich culture of North Macedonia is evidenced in its well-preserved customs, epic poetry, legends, colorful costumes, wonderful folklore and memorable music, which are considered the best features of the Balkans. The culture of the North-Macedonian people is characterized in both traditionalist and modernist attributes. Traces of the antiquity of North Macedonia are still clearly visible today in archaeological sites of Stobi in Veles, Scupi in Skopje, Stibera in Prilep, Heraclea in Bitola, the antique theater in Ohrid…. Culture of Macedonians is strongly bond with their native land and the surrounding in which they live. The rich cultural heritage of the Macedonians is accented in the folklore, the picturesque traditional folk costumes, decorations and ornaments in city and village homes, the architecture, the monasteries and churches, iconostasis, wood-carving and so on. The culture of

Macedonians can roughly be explained as a Balkanic, closely related to that of Serbs and Bulgarians.

By the act of planned settlement of the Kosovo Vilayet and the borders with Serbia by the Albanians and Muslem people, the Porte wanted to disrupt unity of Serbia and surrounding territories settled by the Serbs, on which it paid right after the Berlin Congress, in the first side on the national territories of Stara Srbija Old Serbia and Macedonia. The present North Macedonia was created on the territory of Stara Srbija Old Serbia, which is possessed by the former Kingdom of Serbia, as per all geoletry documents on this millennia territory that Serbia possesses, since the early Middle ages, up to the AVNOJ /*Antifašističko veće narodnog oslobođenja Jugoslavije*/ the Anti-Fascist Council for the National Liberation of Yugoslavia. On this territory the nation had been created from the Serbs by using the name of the Greek geographic area, which was in 1945 granted by creation of the language by the Serb Blaže Koneski Blagoje Ljamević.

On 8th October 1331 Dusan Nemanjic was crowned and set on the Serbian throne. The Serbian state reached its pinnacle in every sense during his reign. Social life was rich, and its dynamics was most expressed in the center of the Dusan's Empire in Kosovo and Metohija and Macedonia. Prizren, Skopje and Ser were towns most frequently visited by the emperor Dusan, who actually ruled from Skopje. Numerous monasteries, churches, and fortress bear witness on the magnificence of Emperor Dusan's reign… and their frescoes depict numerous Serbian rulers and nobility. Slava patron saint is the unique customs of the Serbs, which is not practiced by any other nation. Celebration of Slava marks the day when the family ancestor received Christianity. By conveying this habit in Macedonia, Serbs remain faithful to their origins. Despite the wide propaganda of Bulgaria and Greece, nearly all Christian population of Macedonia had preserved the habit of celebration of the slava feast, which defines their Serbian origins, regardless the nation they belonged during the Turkish rule. Slava was celebrated by a small feast, even in wars, and while detained in prison, and when boots needed to be sold, to provide a tiny and poor outcome....

It is said and still is strongly widely believed that inhabitants of the southern parts had always loved the sun. It was known that sun warms all people and provide life, so in time those areas were recognized as the countries of sun...

There are many cultural traits of people of Macedonia, of which one is celebration of the Orthodox Christmas. The Macedonian Orthodox Christmas celebration begins the evening of January 5th, which is known as "Kolede". Children go from door to door singing Christmas carols, heralding the birth of Jesus, and receiving fruits, nuts and candy from the people. Later in the evening, the elderly people from the neighborhood gather around a bonfire outside, and engage in a conversation about the past year and the year to come.

Rich culture of Macedonian people is vivid in well preserved customs, among which is the Orthodox Christmas Eve, when a traditional oak log (badnik) is brought to the home. This log is cut by the father of the household and his older son, while the table is being set for the Christmas Eve supper (Posna Vechera). The dinner cannot have anything derived from animals, and it cannot be cooked using cooking oil or other types of fat. The traditional dinner usually consists of baked fish. The dinner is the last day of a traditional 40-day Orthodox Lent, which is done in a way to honor the Virgin Mary for carrying baby Jesus. The oak log is cut into three pieces, representing the Holy Trinity, and each piece is brought into the house by the father. A member of the family receives a piece and places it on the fire. As this is done, the son and the father exchange a greeting: "Good evening and happy Christmas Eve"

(Dobra Vecher i Vesel Badnik). While the log is being placed on the fire, the mother and the grandmother gather the children together into the room where the dinner is to be served. Each person carries a bundle of straw from outside, and together with the mother they spread the straw on the floor. The spreading of the straw on the house floor is meant to make the atmosphere more like that when the night Jesus was born. The house is decorated further with oak and pine branches, representing the wish of the family for long and healthy life, "with health strong as oak, and with a life long as that of the oak."

Macedonian National Museum & Icon Gallery Skopje

National Museum of Macedonia in Skopje is divided into three departments: Archeological, Historical, and Ethnological (the same ticket covers them all). It is highly advised to visit the Ethnological section of the National Museum of Macedonia, since it is a very good one. The Ethnological section exposes about 70 original national costumes from different parts of Macedonia, all decorated with highly stylized and wonderful patterns. Look for the *Wedding dress from Mavrovo,* which is 40 kg in weight, and the wig that the bride had to wear for a month after the wedding as a symbol of her virginity. Also different customs are explained, and there is also a good presentation of traditional architecture through models and photographs. The archaeological section of the National Museum of Macedonia in Skopje has a rich collection of objects from the neolithic times 5000 years B.C. up to the 7th century A.D. Unfortunately many artifacts have been taken to Belgrade or Sofia through the years and they have never been returned. The highlights are the Tetovo Menada figurine (from the 6th century BC) and the prehistoric figurines of the Great Mother. Unique are the 6th century terracotta icons from Vinica (icons like this have been found only in Tunisia and Macedonia). The historic department is not as interesting, but also presented here are copies of the best frescoes from all around Macedonia (which is good if one is interested in Byzantine art but does not have time to travel around). The gallery of icons is also here, it comprises icons from the 10th to the 19th century, and even some of them are the best ones from Macedonia (including the Bogorodica Pelagonitisa), but the Ohrid Icon collection is still much nicer and more valuable.

The movie was directed by Milcho Manchevski and shot in London and in remote Macedonian region of Mariovo, among the rocky plateaus and stone houses of two beautiful if mostly deserted villages Štavica and Zovik. The "Before the Rain" movie was nominated for an Academy Award and won the Golden Lion in Venice and features music by Anastasia a blend combining Byzantine past, Orthodox Church music and a rich gamut of ethnic Macedonian rhythms....

The circularity of violence seen in a story that circles on itself. In Macedonia, during war in Bosnia, Macedonians (Christians) hunt an ethnic Albanian (Muslim) girl who may have murdered one of their own. A young monk (Kiril) who's taken a vow of silence offers her protection. In London, a photographic editor who's pregnant needs to talk it out with her estranged husband and chooses a toney restaurant. She wants permanence with her lover, a prize-winning Macedonian photographer just back from Bosnia, changed by the violence he saw and felt there. He leaves abruptly for his village; he's not visited it in 16 years. There he tries to ignore bitter divisions between his Macedonian Orthodox brethren and local Albanian Muslims, then tries to transcend them.

Macedonian Music

The Macedonian music is extremely singable and always awake emotions of every person who listens it.... Macedonian Music that follows traditional dances is very strong and so amazing that make you fall in love in every song.... Macedonian dances are very dynamic and provide its listener and auditorium to feel and learn events of past, performed to present the most beautiful gems of Macedonia's folk treasury. Macedonian traditional dances have important place in the folklore and the music traditions of Macedonia. Macedonian folklore best describes the strongly positive and highly sensitive soul of people of Macedonia. The folklore dances of Macedonia include those dances connected with life cycles and could be defined as the warrior, wedding, harvest, love dances and others....

Great effort has been invested in the support of Macedonian language and culture, not only through education but also through theatre and other arts as well as the media of mass communication.

Daily life and social customs

As a result of the long presence of the Ottoman Turks in the region, the traditional cuisine of North Macedonia is not only based on Balkan and Mediterranean fare but also flavoured by Turkish influences. Among the country's dishes of Turkish origin are kebapcinja (grilled beef kebabs) and the burek, a flaky pastry often stuffed with cheese, meat, or spinach. Macedonians also enjoy other foods that are common throughout the Balkans, including taratur (yogurt with shredded cucumber) and baklava. Macedonian specialties include ajvar (a sauce made from sweet red peppers), tavce gravce (baked beans), shopska salata (a salad combining sliced cucumbers, onions, and tomatoes with soft white cheese), and selsko meso (pork chops and mushrooms in brown gravy).

In addition to Orthodox Christian and Islamic religious holidays, a number of holidays tied to the country's history are celebrated in North Macedonia, including Independence Day (September 8), marking the day in 1991 when Macedonians voted for independence from federated Yugoslavia.

The arts

Despite the refusal of Macedonia's Serbian rulers to recognize Macedonian as a language, progress was made toward the foundation of a national language and literature in the early 20th century, especially by Krste P. Misirkov in his Za Makedonskite raboti (1903; "In Favour of Macedonian Literary Works") and in the literary periodical Vardar (established 1905). These efforts were continued during the interval between World War I and World War II, most notably by the poet Kosta Racin. After World War II, Macedonia freed to write and publish in its own language produced such literary figures as poets Aco Šopov, Slavko Janevski, Blae Koneski, and Gane Todorovski. Janevski also authored the first Macedonian novel, Selo zad sedumte jaseni (1952; "The Village Beyond the Seven Ash Trees"), and a cycle of six novels dealing with Macedonian history. After World War II, Macedonian theatre was invigorated by a wave of new dramatists that included Kole Čašule, Tome Arsovski, and Goran Stefanovski. Among the best-known fiction writers of prose are Živko Čingo, Vlada Urošević, and Jovan Pavlovski. (See Macedonian literature).

The popular culture of North Macedonia is a fascinating blend of local tradition and imported influence. Folk music and folk dancing are still popular, and rock and pop music are ubiquitous. Icon painting and wood carving both have long histories in North Macedonia. Motion picture making in North Macedonia dates to the early 20th-century efforts of brothers Milton and Janaki Manaki and includes Before the Rain (1994), which was directed by Milcho Manchevski and was nominated for an Academy Award for best foreign-language film.

Cultural institutions

Located in Ohrid, the National Museum features an archaeological collection dating from prehistoric times. Ohrid itself is one of the oldest human settlements in Europe, and the natural and cultural heritage of the Ohrid region was designated as a UNESCO World Heritage site in 1980. Also of note are the Museum of Contemporary Art in Skopje and the Museum of the City of Skopje.

Throughout the country, annual festivals are held, including the Skopje Jazz Festival, the Balkan Festival of Folk Songs and Dances in Ohrid, the Ohrid Summer Festival, and the pre-Lenten Carnival in Strumica. An international poetry festival is held annually in the lakeside resort of Struga.

Sports and recreation

A modern sports culture was slow to develop in North Macedonia. In the post-World War II era, football (soccer) emerged as a popular sport, encouraged, along with basketball and volleyball, by the larger industrial firms, which often fielded their own teams. In the late 20th and early 21st centuries, tennis began to grow in popularity in the larger urban centres. The 1996 Olympic Games in Atlanta, Georgia, U.S., marked the first Games at which Macedonia was represented as an independent state.

During the 1970s, winter sports gained considerably in popularity in North Macedonia, as the country's mountainous terrain facilitated the creation of several ski resorts, especially in the Šar Mountains, and near Mavrovo and Krushevo. There are also active mountaineering societies, maintaining huts in the Babuna massif south of Skopje, in the Šar Mountains, and on Baba Mountain. Macedonians generally seem to prefer to take their fresh air and exercise in the form of mountaineering and hunting. On the other hand, chess has a wide and enthusiastic following in the country.

Media and publishing

The Macedonian Information Agency (MIA), which provides news and public information, was originally chartered by the parliament in 1992 but did not begin operation until 1998. In 2006 the government transformed the MIA from public enterprise to joint-stock company. Founded in 1992, Makfax was the region's first private news agency. Although private competitors exist, the major provider of radio and television service is the government-operated Macedonia Radio Television, which began life as Radio Skopje in 1944.

Gastronomy of Macedonia

North Macedonia's favorable warm climate with predominantly pleasant Mediterranean influence coming along the Balkan river valleys featuring finest waters and fertile soil and plenty of benefitial sunshine /Ohrid has 2300 sunny hours per year/ provide fruitful harvests of juicy and delicious fruits and vegetables and *wonderful traditional produces*. Macedonian food is one of the most delicious foods in the world. The secret of its irreplaceable flavor is that it's been prepared the same way for centuries: with lots of love. Some food recipes in North Macedonia have been restored and adapted to the present day. Macedonian cuisine is one of the most popular cuisines in the Balkans, reflecting the Mediterranean and the Middle Eastern influences and shares characteristics of other Balkan cuisines. North Macedonia is also rich in extraordinary quality of meat delicacies, producing *beef, chicken, pork and lamb, and a whole range of game*. Macedonian cuisine is also known for the variety and large quantities of dairy products, fantastic *dough dishes and pastries* for which Macedonians are true masters, as well as for varied local alcoholic drinks like rakija and various wines and liquors.

The agricultural sector in North Macedonia represents a significant area due to the fact that agriculture it employs a relevant number of the population; it is identified as one of the strategic as well as highly potential sector. In fact, few countries as small as Macedonia can offer such variety of products including everything from citrus fruits, grapes, almonds and hazelnuts to excellent tobacco, rice and various mountain teas. Harvesting and processing of wild eco products (forest fruits, mushrooms and medicinal herbs) is also developing in some areas of wonderful North Macedonia.

Macedonia is especially well known for its high quality and delicious *cheeses*: soft white cheese (sirenje), similar to Greek feta, yellow cheese (*kashkaval*) similar to Italian Locatello Romano and also its yoghurt and milk. Every North Macedonian village offers unique and tasty local varieties of cheese.

Among the most popular vegetables in Macedonia are the red peppers, so *there are more than 1000 traditional recipes with or including pepper in North Macedonia* ! Every Macedonian garden grows red peppers, often very hot, sometimes just mild. The unique and specific decorative sight of red peppers, hung out to dry on every veranda for use in winter cooking, is found everywhere in North Macedonia. In autumn in Macedonia peppers are picked, roasted, skinned, pulped and produces into the *ayvar,* the most popular Balkan appetizer-relish and the best red pepper paste you can find. North Macedonia is famous exporter of fresh and processed, pasteurized and pickled vegetables, packed in cans and glass jars, such are *peppers, red peppers, ajvar, lutenica, pindjur, cabbage leaves, apple peppers, roasted peppers, hot peppers, pfefferoni, beet root, green tomato, plum sweet preserve, small baby cucumbers gherkins, cauliflower, carrots, eggplant…..*

Gourmands claim that "gravče na tavče" dish can be compared with truffles, oysters and caviar, and that the quality of the Macedonian beans prepared in clay pots gives the "gravce na tavce" Macedonian traditional specialty the distinctive savor. Variety of delicious traditional specialties are offered for memorable food enjoyment in

Macedonia, especially for religious holidays and celebration of Easter and Christmas, when table is uniquely rich and tasty : Turli tava, lutenica, Banitza-Spinach Pie-Zelnik, Pastrmajlija rustic bread pie, Selsko meso meat chunks slowly stewed in clay pot with whatever vegetables are available in the kitchen, such as onions, tomatoes, carrots, and potatoes, Tarator, Old Pie with white cheese, Ohrid and Pelister trout, gjomleze dish, stuffed peppers, moussaka, vine leaves sarma,... Likewise in the whole Balkans, here the skilled hands of Macedonians sincerely compete with their regional neighbors about whose sweets are the best quality *baklava* and other authentic and usually homemade-style sweet products. Orchards and farms of Macedonia provide abundance of fresh fruits and exceptionally tasty vegetables all year round.

Viticulture in Macedonia is very rich and varied in potential for grape growing, since the country has a long and distinguished history of wine-making. Macedonian wines are among the best in the world, thanks to abundance of beneficial sun in Macedonia throughout the year. The story of the Macedonian wines is cordial, friendly and colorful, since grapes have been cultivated and excellent wine have been produced in the most fertile regions of Macedonia along the course of the Vardar River, bathed in the heat of the sun. Whole families, in several regions in Macedonia taken by the power of wine, for generations now, from father to son, have conveyed the story of the healing power of the God's drink and continue the tradition of grapes cultivation. After tobacco, wine is the second largest agricultural export from North Macedonia. There are more than *80 wineries currently in North Macedonia,* out of which *25 are successful exporters of wine* in the world market. The intense aromas, complex fullness and fantastic quality of the Macedonian wines come from the combined influence of specific soil fertility, and the Mediterranean and continental climates featuring warm summer days and cooler nights. Macedonia produces all sorts of wine dry and sweet, still and sparkling, red, white and rose.

Today North Macedonia has around 24,000 hectares of vineyards that produce considerable quantities of highest quality grape. The two main varieties grown in North Macedonia are Vranec (red) and Smederevka (white). Beside those two the most popular, varieties include international ones like Merlot, Cabernet Sauvignon, and Pinot Noir from the red and Chardonnay, Riesling, and Sauvignon Blanc from the white varieties. In addition there are number of other different varieties as Muscat Ottonel, Semillon, Rkaciteli, Grenache Blanc, and Kadarka, that are grown in Macedonia.

While you travel down the course of the Vardar River in North Macedonia the grape fields follow you at you every step. There are grape fields and vineyards in the regions of Skopje, Veles, Gevgelija-Valandovo, Strumica, Ovcepolje, Kocani-Vinica, Ohrid, Prilep, Bitola /Pelagonija-Polosko region/, Prespa, Kicevo, Tetovo and Pcinja Osogovo. The most recognizable and famous wine area in Macedonia is the Tikvesh wine region, and its center Kavadarci and Negotino are the biggest producers of the heady liquid of fantastic wines. Tikvesh wines reflect over 120 years of a culture which celebrates the entire wine experience and is must !

OHRID CHOMLEK Recipe

Chomlek is traditional North Macedonian stew typically prepared in clay pots with veal or baby beef and plenty of onions, garlic and herbs. Prepared in Pelagonija and southwest of North Macedonia, towns of Bitola, Prilep, Ohrid, and Krushevo with slightly different own versions and ingredients of this tasty dish.

Ingredients for 4 persons of Ohrid Chomlek : 800 gr beef boneless, 6 cloves of garlic, 800 gr onions, salt, peppercorn, 1 spoon of red paprika powder, 2 spoons of oil, 2 spoons of vinegar

Preparation of Macedonian /Ohrid/ chomlek : Cut met into larger pieces. Slice onions and chop garlic. If onions are small, use whole onions without slicing or slice them in quarters. Lay layers of meat in ceramic pot and cover them with layers of sliced onions and garlic until the top of the pot and all ingredients used. Add salt, red paprika powder, pepper, oil, vinegar and water to fill the top of the pot. Cook on medium heat until meat becomes tender and almost all water is dried. Serve Chomlek with warm homemade buns.

SHEPHERD SARMA"

Cabbage casserole Shepherd original dish :

Ingredients : 500 gr of cut pickled sauerkraut, 600 gr minced mixed veal and pork meat, 1 onion, 100 gr rice, 1 garlic, small spoon of salt, half of a small spoon of cracked black pepper, half of a small spoon of cooking dried vegetable spice, 1 kg of potato, 500 gr sour cream, 3 eggs

Preparation : cook potato in boiled water and mash it. Ad sour cream, salt and chopped garlic, 2 yolks and whisked egg whites. Fry chopped onion on little oil, add minced meat and continue frying for 10-15 minutes. Wash pickled cabbage sauerkaut in water to avoid too sour taste it originally has. Boil race for some 10 minutes. Mash all meat, rice, chopped onion, spice and stir all well. Cover the griddle pan with butter and put the layer of cut sauerkraut, and some 150 ml of water. Cover this layer with the mixture of meat and ride and eggs and make it even. Make the next layer of tomato above it and bake the dish for 45 minutes On the temperature of 175 C. Serve the baked Shepherd Sarma in the same dish in which it was cooked.

KRATOVO PASTRAMAJLIJA or KRATOVO PASTRMAJKA

Pastrmajlija or pastrmajka is Rustic Bread Pie Savory pie from Kratovo. It differs a bit in taste from the other pastrmajlija varieties

of Macedonia such as Veleshka pita pie or Shtipska pastrmajlija by use of smoked pork delicacies instead of the usual pork and cured lamb or sheep meat. It is assumed that the name comes from smoked sheep meat called pastrma, *although this type of meat was not frequently used in preparation of pastrmajlija.*

Ingredients :

For the dough: 300 gr of white flour, 30 gr of Yeast, salt, sugar and water
For the filling: about 250gr smoked ham, optionally may be added 1 egg
Preparation first make dough of flour, yeast, salt and sugar and water. Knead the dough well and leave it on side for about an hour to grow up to double quantity and rest well. After that roll the dough in "pastrmajka"elongated and ellipsoid form, fill it with smoked meat or whatever ingredients available and leave for a while for some time for additional rest, add little fat-grease over the filling and then bake it in pre- heated oven at 300 degrees. Serve the Kratovo Pastrmajlija with popular Kratovo red wine. !

History of North Macedonia

As described in this article's introduction, the name Macedonia is applied both to a region encompassing the present-day Republic of North Macedonia and portions of Bulgaria and Greece and to the republic itself, the boundaries of which have been defined since 1913. In the following discussion, the name Macedonia is used generally to describe the larger region prior to 1913 and the area of the present-day republic thereafter.

The ancient world

The Macedonian region has been the site of human habitation for millennia. There is archaeological evidence that the Old European

(Neolithic) civilization flourished there between 7000 and 3500 BCE. Seminomadic peoples speaking languages of the Indo-European family then moved into the Balkan Peninsula. During the 1st millennium BCE the Macedonian region was populated by a mixture of peoples Dacians, Thracians, Illyrians, Celts, and Greeks. Although Macedonia is most closely identified historically with the kingdom of Philip II of Macedon in the middle of the 4th century BCE and the subsequent expansion of that empire by his son Alexander III (the Great), none of the states established in that era was very durable. Until the arrival of the Romans, the pattern of politics was a shifting succession of contending city-states and chiefdoms that occasionally integrated into ephemeral empires. Nevertheless, this period is important in understanding the present-day region, as both Greeks and Albanians base their claims to be indigenous inhabitants of it on the achievements of the Macedonian and Illyrian states.

At the end of the 3rd century BCE, the Romans began to expand into the Balkan Peninsula in search of metal ores, slaves, and agricultural produce. The Illyrians were finally subdued in 9 CE (their lands becoming the province of Illyricum), and the north and east of Macedonia were incorporated into the province of Moesia in 29 CE. A substantial number of sites bear witness today to the power of Rome, especially Heraclea Lyncestis (modern Bitola) and Stobi (south of Veles on the Vardar River). The name Skopje is Roman in origin (Scupi). Many roads still follow courses laid down by the Romans.

Beginning in the 3rd century, the defenses of the Roman Empire in the Balkans were probed by Goths, Huns, Bulgars, Avars, and other seminomadic peoples. Although the region was nominally a part of the Eastern Empire, control from Constantinople became more and more intermittent. By the mid-6th century Slavic tribes had begun to settle in Macedonia, and from the 7th to the 13th century the entire region was little more than a system of military marches governed uneasily by the Byzantine state through alliances with local princes.

The medieval states

In the medieval period the foundations were laid for modern competing claims for control over Macedonia. During the 9th century the Eastern tradition of Christianity was consolidated in the area. The mission to the Slavs has come to be associated with Saints Cyril and Methodius, whose great achievement was the devising of an alphabet based on Greek letters and adapted to the phonetic peculiarities of the Slavonic tongue. In its later development as the Cyrillic alphabet, this came to be a distinctive cultural feature uniting several of the Slavic peoples.

Although the central purpose of the missionaries was to preach the Gospel to the Slavs in the vernacular, their ecclesiastical connection with the Greek culture of Constantinople remained a powerful lever to be worked vigorously during the struggle for Macedonia in the 19th century. About three-fourths of the inhabitants of the present-day Republic of North Macedonia have a Macedonian national identity. They are Slavic-speaking descendants of the Slavic tribes who have lived in the area since the 6th century. The long association of the area with the Greek-speaking Byzantine state, and the Greek claim to continuity with the ancient Macedonian empire of Alexander the Great, led the Greek state to claim that "Macedonia was, is, and always will be Greek." Since the independence of the Republic of Macedonia in 1991, Greece on these grounds attempted to block the international recognition of the Republic of Macedonia by its constitutional name and to deny the Macedonians of the Republic of Macedonia and Greece the right to identify themselves as Macedonians.

What is less clear is the history of the emergence of a Macedonian national identity from a more general identity as Slavic-speaking Orthodox Christians as well as from a Bulgarian national identity, the latter of which developed before a Macedonian identity did. Among the short-lived states jostling for position with Byzantium were two that modern Bulgarians claim give them a special stake in Macedonia. Under the reign of Simeon I (893–927), Bulgaria emerged briefly as the dominant power in the peninsula, extending its control from the Black Sea to the Adriatic. Following a revolt of the western provinces, this first Bulgarian empire fell apart, but it was partially reintegrated by Samuel (reigned 976–1014), who set up his own capital in Ohrid (not the traditional Bulgarian capital of Preslav [now known as Veliki Preslav]) and also established a patriarchate there. Although the Byzantine state reasserted its authority after 1018, a second Bulgarian empire raised its head in 1185; this included northern and central Macedonia and lasted until the mid-14th century.

During the second half of the 12th century, a more significant rival to Byzantine power in the Balkans emerged in the Serbian Nemanjić dynasty. Stefan Nemanja became veliki župan, or "grand chieftain," of Raška in 1169, and his successors created a state that under Stefan Dušan (reigned 1331–55) incorporated Thessaly, Epirus, Macedonia, all of modern Albania and Montenegro, a substantial part of Bosnia, and Serbia as far north as the Danube. Although the cultural heart of the empire was Raška (the area around modern Novi Pazar) and Kosovo, as the large number of medieval Orthodox churches in those regions bear witness, Stefan Dušan was crowned emperor in Skopje in 1346. Within half a century after his death, the Nemanjić state was eclipsed by the expanding Ottoman Empire; nevertheless, it is to this golden age that Serbs today trace their own claims to Macedonia.

The Ottoman Empire

The Ottoman Empire originated in a small emirate established in the second half of the 13th century in northwestern Anatolia. By 1354 it had gained a toehold in Europe, and by 1362 Adrianople (modern Edirne, Turkey) had fallen. From this base the power of this Turkish and Islamic state steadily expanded. From a military point of view, the most significant defeat of the Serbian states took place in the Battle of the Maritsa River at Chernomen in 1371, but it is the defeat in 1389 of a combined army of Serbs, Albanians, and Hungarians under Lazar at the Battle of Kosovo that has been preserved in legend as symbolizing the subordination of the Balkan Slavs to the "Ottoman yoke." Constantinople itself did not fall to the Ottoman Turks until 1453, but by the end of the 14th century the Macedonian region had been incorporated into the Ottoman Empire. Thus began what was in many respects the most stable period of Macedonian history, lasting until the Turks were ejected from the region in 1913.

Half a millennium of contact with Turkey had a profound impact on language, food, and many other aspects of daily life in Macedonia. Within the empire, administrators, soldiers, merchants, and artisans moved in pursuit of their professions. Where war, famine, or disease left regions underpopulated, settlers were moved in from elsewhere with no regard for any link between ethnicity and territory. By the system known as devşirme (the notorious "blood tax"), numbers of Christian children were periodically recruited into the Turkish army and administration, where they were Islamized and assigned to wherever their services were required. For all these reasons, many Balkan towns acquired a cosmopolitan atmosphere. This was particularly the case in Macedonia during the 19th century, when, as the Serbian, Greek, and Bulgarian states began to assert their independence, many who had become associated with Turkish rule moved into lands still held by the Sublime Porte.

The economic legacy of Turkish rule is also important. During the expansionist phase of the empire, Turkish feudalism consisted principally of the timar system of "tax farming," whereby local officeholders raised revenue or supported troops in the sultan's name but were not landowners. As the distinctively military aspects of the Ottoman order declined after the 18th century, these privileges were gradually transformed in some areas into the çiftlik system, which more closely resembled proprietorship over land. This process involved the severing of the peasantry from their traditional rights on the land and a corresponding creation of large estates farmed on a commercial basis. The çiftlik thus yielded the paradox of a population that was heavily influenced by Ottoman culture yet bound into an increasingly oppressive economic subordination to Turkish landlords.

The independence movement

Conflict and confusion deepened in Macedonia in the closing decades of the 19th century. As the Turkish empire decayed, Serbia, Greece, and Bulgaria all looked to benefit territorially from the approaching division of Macedonia that would inevitably follow the end of Ottoman rule. At the same time, these three states each became stalking horses for the aspirations of the European great powers. The weapons employed in this conflict ranged widely; they included opening schools and churches in an attempt to inculcate a particular linguistic and confessional identity, exerting influence over the course of railway lines, diplomatic attempts to secure the ear of the Sublime Porte, and even financing guerrilla bands.

Partly in response to the intensity of these campaigns of pressure and even terror, a movement called the Internal Macedonian Revolutionary Organization (IMRO) was founded in 1893, at Resana (Resen) near Ohrid. The aim of IMRO was "Macedonia for the Macedonians," and on July 20 (August 2, New Style), 1903, it raised the banner of revolt against the Turks at Kruševo and declared Macedonian independence. The Ilinden, or St. Elijah's Day, Uprising was quickly and brutally crushed. One of IMRO's leaders, Gotsé Delchev, whose nom de guerre was Ahil (Achilles), is regarded by both Macedonians and Bulgarians as a national hero. He seems to have identified himself as a Bulgarian and to have regarded the Slavs of Macedonia as Bulgarians. He died and was buried in what is now northern Greece in 1903. During World War I he was reburied in Bulgaria, and then in 1946 his remains were moved again, this time to Skopje, where his body remained. From this period at the beginning of the 20th century, the Macedonian Question has been a major force in Balkan history and politics.

War and partition

In spite of their conflicting interests, in 1912 Serbia, Montenegro, Greece, and Bulgaria concluded a series of secret bilateral treaties that had the explicit intention of ejecting the Ottoman Turks from Europe. They took advantage of an uprising by the Albanian population to intervene in October 1912 and, following their defeat of the sultan's armies in the first of the Balkan Wars, partitioned the remaining Turkish possessions (including Macedonia) among them. The Treaty of London (May 1913), which concluded this First Balkan War, left Bulgaria dissatisfied, but, after that country's attempt to enforce a new partition in a Second Balkan War, the Treaty of Bucharest (August 1913) confirmed a pattern of boundaries that (with small variations) has remained in force ever since. Although the region was again engulfed in conflict during World War I, and Bulgaria occupied large parts of Macedonia, the partition of 1913 was reconfirmed at the end of war in 1918.

During the interwar years, intensive campaigning took place in all areas of Macedonia to impose identities on the population that suited the interests of the controlling states. In a Serbian attempt to secure northern, or "Vardar," Macedonia's status as South Serbia, the area was subjected to an active Serbian colonization program under land-reform legislation. Following the forcible ejection of Greeks from Turkey during the 1920s, thousands of Greek settlers were given land in southern, or "Aegean," Macedonia. Both Serbia and Greece took advantage of the displacement by war or expulsion of many former Turkish landowners.

During that period a link was consolidated between politicized agricultural labourers (especially tobacco workers) on the large Macedonian estates and the nascent Communist Party a link that survived the proscription of the party in Yugoslavia after 1921. Partly because of its communist associations, the movement for Macedonian independence was then sustained largely underground until the outbreak of World War II.

The republic

When war overtook the Balkans again in 1941, the kingdom of Yugoslavia was again divided, this time between the Axis powers and their allies. Yugoslav Macedonia was occupied principally by Bulgaria, the western part being joined to a united Albania under Italian control. The ethnic complexity of the region, together with its history of division and manipulation by outsiders, left the local population demoralized and conflicted. The need to reconcile communist internationalism with the desire for national self-determination posed problems of extreme political sensitivity for resistance groups. In 1945 the area was reincorporated into Yugoslavia, this time under communist control. In an attempt to correct the mistakes of the first Yugoslavia, in which a heavily centralized regime had been dominated by the Serbian dynasty, administration, and armed forces, the second Yugoslavia was organized as a federation, and Macedonia was established as one of its six constituent republics.

The consolidation of communist control after the expulsion of the Axis powers was relatively rapid and effective in Yugoslavia. In Greece, however, civil war between communist and royalist forces lasted until 1949, when, under international pressure, Yugoslavia agreed to end its support for the Greek guerrillas. Because of the close ties between Macedonian communists in Yugoslavia and ethnic Macedonians in Greece, thousands of Macedonians fled Greece both during and after the Greek Civil War of 1946–49.

The autonomy of the republic was perhaps more cosmetic than real, although great efforts were made to support a sense of national identity among Macedonians. A Macedonian language was codified and disseminated through the educational system (including the first Macedonian university), the mass media, and the arts. An important symbol of the existence of a Macedonian nation was the creation of an autocephalous Macedonian Orthodox Church. Since the 1890s a great deal of dissatisfaction had been expressed in Macedonia with the unsympathetic attitude of the Serbian church, with which Orthodox Macedonians had long been affiliated. There is little doubt, however, that their autocephalous status would never have been achieved without the vigorous support of the League of Communists of Yugoslavia. The archbishopric of Ohrid was restored in 1958, and autocephaly was declared in 1967. Although national churches are typical in the Orthodox communion, in the case of the Macedonians it became the root of a great deal of hostility on the part of neighbouring Orthodox peoples. The Macedonian Orthodox Church is not recognized by the patriarch or by any other Orthodox church.

Macedonia's economic development lagged behind that of the more-developed republics throughout the communist period, yet Macedonians remained among the most loyal supporters of the Yugoslav federation, which seemed to offer their best guarantee against claims on their territory by other countries and against secessionist sentiments on the part of internal minorities. This loyalty survived the strain both of the suppression of nationalism by Yugoslav federal authorities and of disputes over republican autonomy between 1968 and 1974. Macedonian politicians persistently sought to broker solutions to the final constitutional crisis and to the breakup of the League of Communists and the Yugoslav federation itself after 1989.

Independence of North Macedonia

In contrast to the other Yugoslav republics, whose efforts to secede from Yugoslavia provoked campaigns of nationalist violence and ethnic cleansing in the early 1990s, the Republic of Macedonia was peacefully established as a sovereign and independent state on September 8, 1991, by a vote of the citizens of Macedonia. Since then Macedonia has faced many serious challenges on both the domestic and international fronts. Conflict with the Albanian minority and the dispute with Greece over the name Macedonia combined to pose significant threats to much-needed foreign investment and economic growth. Moreover, while overseeing the demanding transition to a free-market economy, a succession of Macedonian governments were bedeviled by corruption and forced to combat organized crime.

More importantly, however, the Macedonian government has been faced with the challenge of maintaining peaceful relations between the country's Orthodox Christian Macedonian majority and a Muslim Albanian minority that constitutes approximately one-fourth of the population. A key issue that has proven difficult to resolve has been balancing Macedonian nationals' commitment to the preservation of a Macedonian state with Albanians' demands for the full rights of citizenship.

According to the original preamble of the 1991 constitution, the Republic of Macedonia was established as "a national state of the

Macedonian people in which full equality as citizens and permanent coexistence with the Macedonian people is provided for Albanians, Turks, Vlachs, Romanies [Roma], and other nationalities." As a result of long-standing Albanian grievances over their status as second-class citizens in the republic and the Albanian insurgency in the northwest of the country that followed the NATO defeat of Slobodan Milošević's Serbia in the Kosovo conflict, in 2001 the preamble of the Macedonian constitution was recast to reflect a more pluralist perspective, referring to "the citizens of the Republic of Macedonia, the Macedonian people, as well as citizens living within its borders who are part of the Albanian people, the Turkish people, the Vlach [Aromani] people, the Serbian people, the Romany people, the Bosniak people."

Kiro Gligorov, a well-respected veteran of many years of service in the Yugoslav federal government, deftly guided the republic through its difficult early years as its first president. A member of the moderate Social Democratic Union of Macedonia (SDSM), which consisted of former communists and social democrats, he was seriously wounded in an assassination attempt in 1995. After having turned over the reigns of power to an acting president for six weeks, he resumed his duties and served as president until 1999. That year power shifted to the right, and Boris Trajkovski of the more nationalist Internal Macedonian Revolutionary Organization–Democratic Party for Macedonian National Unity (VMRO-DPMNE) came to power. In 2004 the presidency shifted to the SDSM, to Branko Crvenkovski, then in 2009 back to the VMRO-DPMNE in the person of Gjorge Ivanov. Historically, the Albanian minority has voted as a bloc for ethnic Albanian parties, and all governments since independence have been coalitions that included an Albanian party.

In early parliamentary elections in June 2011, the VMRO-DPMNE-led coalition finished first with 39 percent of the vote but, having captured 56 seats, fell short of an outright majority. Nonetheless, Nikola Gruevski renewed his governing coalition with the ethnic-Albanian Democratic Union for Integration (BDI), which took more than 10 percent of the vote and 15 seats. By garnering nearly 33 percent of the vote, the SDSM increased its representation considerably to 42 seats. Two other ethnic-Albanian parties also made their mark: the Democratic Party of Albanians (PDSh), with almost 6 percent of the vote and 8 seats, and the newly formed National Democratic Revival (RK), with about 3 percent and 2 seats. This proved to be a period of extensive political turmoil, which included a prolonged boycott of the parliament by the SDSM.

Under the EU-mediated agreement that was reached on March 1, 2013, the SDSM returned to the parliament and agreed to participate in the local elections in return for discussions about possible parliamentary elections later in the year and the formation of a special parliamentary committee to investigate the events of December 24, 2012. On that day SDSM MPs had tried to literally block the adoption of the state budget by surrounding the speaker of the parliament's desk. After they were forcibly removed from the legislature, the ruling VMRO-DPMNE passed the budget by a vote of 64–4, and the SDSM began its boycott of the parliament.

In response to SDSM demands, changes were made to the election code, and an agreement was reached to clean up the voter register. Those changes set the stage for elections in April 2014, in which Ivanov was reelected president and the VMRO-DPMNE maintained control of the parliament by capturing 42.2 percent of the vote and 61 of the body's 123 seats. The SDSM-led coalition won 24.9 percent of the vote and 34 seats; the BDI finished third with 13.5 percent and 19 seats. International observers acknowledged the efficient administration of the elections but criticized what they saw as the lack of separation between state and ruling party. Most SDSM MPs, claiming that fraud had been committed by the government and the ruling parties, again chose not to take up their seats in the parliament. Nevertheless, in June, Gruevski's new government made up of the VMRO-DPMNE, its smaller ethnic-Macedonian partner parties, and the BDI received a vote of confidence in the parliament.

In early 2015 the opposition alleged that Gruevski and his intelligence chief had initiated the wiretapping of some 670,000 conversations on about 20,000 telephones from 2007 to 2013. The opposition also began releasing snippets of the recorded conversations that it said had been leaked by civil servants. The recordings painted a picture of a VMRO-DPMNE awash in corruption. In the process, a firestorm of political turmoil overwhelmed the country and forced Gruevski's resignation in January 2016 as part of an EU-brokered deal that set the stage for early elections to be held in April. Emil Dimitriev took over as caretaker prime minister. After being postponed twice, the elections were held in December 2016.

In the event, the VMRO-DPMNE appeared to have beaten the SDSM by just over 300 votes in the country's sixth district. Had that result stood, the VMRO-DPMNE would have held 51 seats in the 120-seat parliament (to 49 for the SDSM) and been positioned to form a coalition government. However, voting irregularities in the village of Tearce meant that its 714 registered voters had to return to the polls on December 25, which raised the possibility that if enough of them voted for the SDSM, the seat count would even out at 50 for each of the two parties. In the event, however, the SDSM still came up short and the VMRO-DPMNE was poised to remain in power. The VMRO-DPMNE, however, was unable to successfully court the coalition partner it needed to continue to govern.

A power vacuum ensued, which appeared to be filled in March 2017 when the SDSM leader Zoran Zaev won the support of ethnic

Albanian parties by promising to support legislation that would extend existing constitutional language rights to make Albanian the country's second official language. (An amendment to the constitution in response to the Ohrid Framework Agreement had made Albanian an official language in communities where Albanian speakers made up at least 20 percent of the population.) President Ivanov initially blocked the formation of the new coalition government but eventually relented to foreign pressure and allowed the new government to be confirmed in office in late May with Zaev as its prime minister. Nevertheless, ethnic tensions remained high. When Talat Xhaferi, an ethnic Albanian, was chosen speaker of the parliament in late April, some 200 Macedonian nationalists invaded parliament and violently attacked lawmakers.

In January 2018 Zaev made good on his promise and introduced a bill to extend Albanian as an official language throughout the country. With the VMRO-DPMNE boycotting the voting, the bill passed with 69 votes in favour. When Ivanov refused to sign the law, parliament voted on it a second time, in March, and passed it again, this time with 64 votes in favour. Although the Macedonian constitution prohibited a president from vetoing legislation that had been approved in two separate votes, Ivanov still refused to sign the legislation, claiming that the proper parliamentary procedure had not been employed in its passage and that the law would "deepen inter-ethnic tensions and represents a threat for the inter-ethnic life."

In 1999, during the Kosovo conflict, more than 350,000 Kosovar Albanian refugees had fled to Macedonia, with significant consequences for the republic. Living standards in Macedonia plummeted, exports declined, and unemployment, already at more than 30 percent before the conflict, rose dramatically to as high as 40–50 percent, according to some estimates. Another serious threat to the country's political stability was posed by an armed conflict that erupted between an ethnic Albanian military group and Macedonian security forces in 2001. This conflict was brought to an end in August 2001 by the signing of the Ohrid Framework Agreement, which contained the government's promises to make Albanian an official language, to increase autonomy for areas with large Albanian populations, and to raise the number of Albanians serving in the army and police as well as in the government. The Macedonian economy gradually recovered with slow but steady GDP growth and minimal inflation until 2009, when it began to struggle in response to the global financial downturn. In the early 2010s the economy again rebounded slowly.

In August 2015 Macedonia became the latest flash point in the migrant crisis that gripped Europe as an increasing number of people fled war and turmoil in the Middle East and Africa. The daily stream of migrants and refugees entering Macedonia swelled from 300–400 in May 2015 to 2,000–3,000 in August, which prompted the Macedonian government to declare a state of emergency on August 21. Human rights groups castigated Macedonia when its police and military used batons, tear gas, and stun grenades the following day in an effort to halt the mass of migrants who attempted to rush into Macedonia across its border with Greece.

By far the greatest challenge for the Republic of Macedonia was Greece's effort to prevent its neighbour from gaining international recognition under its constitutional name, along with blocking Macedonia's participation in international organizations. Greece's attempt to monopolize the name Macedonia prevented the republic from gaining entry into a variety of international organizations and from enjoying the economic and political stability that membership in such organizations would provide. When the Republic of Macedonia declared its independence in 1991, Greece immediately objected to the name of the new republic, insisting that "Macedonia" had been used by Greeks since ancient times and that its "appropriation" by the Republic of Macedonia constituted a "falsification of history" and a revival of territorial claims on Greek Macedonia (Makedonía). The Macedonian republic argued in turn that Slavs had lived in the area for 14 centuries and had used the name Macedonia for hundreds of years.

Responding to the Republic of Macedonia's attempt to gain recognition from the European Community (EC; later the European Union), an EC arbitration commission concluded not only that the newly independent country met all the criteria necessary for recognition but also that its use of the name Macedonia implied no claims on Greek territory the contention of the Greek government. Nevertheless, Greece was able to prevent EC recognition of the republic. Only by acceding to a provisional designation as "the Former Yugoslav Republic of Macedonia" did Macedonia gain admission to the United Nations in 1993.

In early 1994, seemingly turning up the pressure on the republic to relinquish its claims to the name Macedonia, Greece instituted an economic blockade that had dire consequences for Macedonia. In September 1995, with more and more countries inveighing for Greece and Macedonia to come to a settlement, the two signed an Interim Accord. The agreement called for Macedonia to remove the 16-ray Sun or Star of Verghina a symbol of the ancient Macedonian royal family that Greece had claimed as a national symbol from its flag and to renounce all territorial claims on Greek Macedonia in return for Greece's termination of the embargo. Moreover, it was agreed that the "name issue" would be submitted to UN-sponsored mediation. In 2004 the Republic of Macedonia was recognized by the United States under its constitutional name. In 2008, however, Greece violated the Interim Accord by preventing Macedonia from being invited to become a member of the North Atlantic Treaty Organization (NATO), again raising objections to the republic's use of the name Macedonia. Nonetheless, UN-sponsored bilateral negotiations over the name continued.

Finally, in June 2018, Prime Minister Zaev and Greek Prime Minister Alexis Tsipras announced that an agreement (thereafter known as the Prespa Agreement) had been reached under which Macedonia would be known both domestically and internationally as the Republic of North Macedonia (Macedonian: Severna Makedonija). The name change required both amendment of the Macedonian constitution and acceptance by the Greek parliament. The process toward those ends began in September with the Macedonian government holding a "consultative" referendum, which was not legally binding but by which lawmakers agreed to abide. The question posed was "Are you for NATO and EU membership with acceptance of the agreement with Greece?" The VMRO-DPMNE denounced the agreement and called on voters to boycott the referendum. Enough Macedonians stayed away from the polls that those who did participate about 37 percent of eligible voters were far short of the 50 percent turnout required to validate the vote, thus leaving legislators free to follow their conscience. However, more than 90 percent of those who voted in the referendum endorsed the agreement.

The three-stage process of amendment to the Macedonian constitution was initiated on October 19, when the parliament, by an 80–39 vote that reached the required two-thirds approval threshold, authorized the government to begin preparing draft constitutional amendments to be submitted to later votes. On December 3 the language of the draft amendments was approved by a 67–23 vote that satisfied the simple majority requirement of the 120-member parliament at this stage. This result set the stage for a vote on whether the amendments should be adopted, which would require a two-thirds majority for passage. Although the majority of VMRO-DPMNE MPs boycotted that vote, which occurred on January 11, 2019, the amendments required to change the country's name won the consent of 81 MPs, just enough to secure passage. The final step in formal approval of the name change now rested with the Greek parliament. Opposition to the Prespa Agreement prompted the departure of the junior partner in Tsipras's ruling coalition and compelled the Greek prime minister to seek a vote of confidence in his government. Having barely survived that challenge, he brought the agreement to a vote on January 25, and the Greek parliament approved it 153–146, laying the groundwork for Greece to formally remove its objection to Macedonian membership in NATO and thus paving the way for official adoption of Macedonia's new name. In early February the Greek parliament approved the protocol for the accession to NATO of the Republic of North Macedonia, which officially became the country's name on February 12, 2019.

North Macedonia's aspiration to European Union membership received a major setback in October 2019, when France, supported by Denmark and the Netherlands, prevented the European Council from reaching an agreement that would have allowed North Macedonia and Albania to begin formal talks on their accession to the EU. In the wake of the council's decision, a deeply disappointed Zaev called for early parliamentary elections that would allow his country's people to weigh in on its political future. Under a 2015 agreement, general elections in the country were to be preceded by 100 days of caretaker government, instituted to remove doubts regarding potential ballot tampering or the application of political pressure by the party in power. In early January 2020, in advance of the election scheduled for April 12, Zaev resigned as prime minister.

As North Macedonia undertook efforts to halt the spread of the global coronavirus (SARs-CoV-2) pandemic that began in China in late 2019, the April elections had to be postponed. When they were able to be conducted in July, Zaev's Social Democratic Party claimed

46 seats to barely outdistance VMRO-DPMNE, which took 44 seats, thus leaving both parties the opportunity to try to coax enough support from other players to form a ruling coalition. By the middle of August, the Social Democrats had renewed their partnership with the Democratic Union for Integration (DUI), the ethnic Albanian party with whom they had shared coalition rule until Zaev had called the snap election. Together the two parties, along with a member from another ethnic Albanian party, possessed enough seats (62) in parliament to form a majority government. Once again, Zaev became prime minister.

Having successfully guided North Macedonia to membership in NATO in March 2020, Zaev looked forward to overcoming the final obstacles to the country's accession to membership in the EU. To that end, in 2017 his government had signed a bilateral friendship accord with Bulgaria and established a commission composed of historians from both countries who were tasked with resolving disagreements over the "shared history" of the two countries. As the date for start of EU accession talks approached, however, the Bulgarian government circulated a document titled "Explanatory Memorandum on the relationship of the Republic of Bulgaria with the Republic of North Macedonia in the context of the EU enlargement and Association and Stabilization Process," in which it challenged North Macedonia to acknowledge its supposed Bulgarian historical roots and to identify its language as a form of Bulgarian. When that acknowledgment was not forthcoming, in mid-November Bulgaria used its veto to prevent the start of EU accession talks for North Macedonia.

Information Tourism, Sites and Landmarks

The Republic of North Macedonia is small, warm, sunny and beautiful Southeast European country, south of *Serbia* and north of

Greece and west of *Bulgaria*. North Macedonia is one of the hidden gems of the former republic of Yugoslavia and present Balkans, that hides a great cultural, historical geographical value which offers its visitors a unique blend of natural wonders, traditions and cultures, as well as long tradition of *unrivaled hospitality*.

North Macedonia is a natural paradise of mountains, fantastic lakes and rivers, where life moves to a different rhythm amid the sprawling grandeur of rich historical treasures and idyllic villages that have remained practically unchanged for centuries. Wonderful mountains of North Macedonia are exceptional destinations for hiking, suitable for fit and active people with some hiking experience, but also for hikers with good level of fitness who like long and steep ascents and descents, and rugged terrains.

North Macedonia's geographical and cultural position as the bridge between East and West, and the crossroads between the Christian Europe and the mystical Orient, is attested to today in its inhabitants featuring *fascinatingly deep spiritual roots*. The importance of North Macedonia as the state and historical-geographical area is in its strategic position. North Macedonia is together with Serbia, the center of the Balkan Peninsula. The former Yugoslav republic and the present state of North Macedonia is artificial creation of communism. Since the beginning of time Macedonia was part of Serbia, as was the *whole territory of Greece* in the early past. It was not the Macedonians /the Serbs/ who stole the name of the present Macedonia, but the Greeks had stolen the land from the Macedonians the Serbs. There are evidences on the Serb population in Macedonia in the 2nd millennia BC that testify on hidden cultural and historical heritage and truths about the ancient Serbs. Those truths are interwoven in the lyric songs of the Macedonian people that have been recorded in Skopje, Prilep, Ohrid, Kumanovo…. The wonderful Medieval church dedicated to Saint Stephen Sveti Stefan in southeast Macedonia, some 20 km south of Radovis is endowment of Nikola Stanjevic, the duke of Tsar Dusan. Knowing that the Turkish rule will be over and removed from the Balkans, the European countries and the Vatican decided to create a non-Serb nation, to establish a non-Serb state and to proclaim a non-Serb Macedonian Orthodox Church from the Serbs in Macedonia. The Serbian state authorities and the Serbian intellectuals did not prevent this, but assisted in performance of this plan in the Kingdom of Yugoslavia, by creation of the Vardar Banovina and and the Republic of Macedonia within the Socialist Federative Republic of Yugoslavia.

Although just a little country, North Macedonia is a true cradle of culture, holding several antique theaters, thousand of Medieval Monasteries and well preserved Byzantine churches and over 200 Ottoman mosques, in addition to the remains from the early' Christian and Stone Age and even earlier periods of human civilization. Alexander the Great of Macedonia was *one of the greatest army commanders in history,* and with some 43,000 infantry and 5,500 cavalry had changed the face of Europe and Asia forever when created an empire that stretched from the Adriatic Sea to India and Egypt. The Illyrian Paionians, Dardanians and Taulantii, the Thracian Odrysai, Getai and Triballi, together with the prosperous West Pontic Greek cities, all acknowledged the sovereignty of the Phillip II of Macedon and his son Alexander who had established loose personal hegemony over much of the Balkans. In 1977 were excavated spectacular golden tomb that contained earthen remains of several humans of the ancient Macedonian royal family. It was ascertained that in one of the coffins of the royal mausoleum 1 there were remains of Philip II, father of Alexander the Great, while in the tomb 2 some relatives of Alexander the Great, like the King Arideus and his wife Euridice. When the archaeologist Manolis Andronikos started excavations of the mausoleums in Vergina in 1977 he had discovered that four of the tombs were not opened for long time and that they include astonishingly rich treasury. Philip II Filip II was the 18th king of Macedonia /359-336 BC/. He restored the internal peace to his state and conquered the whole Greece in military and diplomatic ways, when he had established foundations for the further extentions which were performed by his son Alexander the Great. Philip II Filip II is described as the powerful king with complicated love life, as he married some 5 to 7 wives, that caused mess in heredity. Filip II Philip II was killed in 336 BC at the wedding ceremony of his daughter, most probably by the order of his former wife Olympia. Alexander the Great inherited the throne from his father and became king.

North Macedonia's cultural richness is expressed in its archaeological legacy of *Heraclea*, *Stobi and Skupi,* strewn with amphitheaters and temples, and decorated with intricate mosaics and frescoes. Positioned on the old Roman caravan road *Via Egnatia* the area of present day North Macedonia provided inspiration for artists and scholars who created magnificent works of art and learning that were to become a glorious legacy for the entire world. UNESCO has recognized the special character of this gorgeous country by designating Ohrid Lake and the City of Ohrid as one of the natural and cultural UNESCO World Heritage Sites.

North Macedonia features 3 national parks, 10 special reservations, 2 regions with exceptional natural beauty, 48 kinds of birds, 55 monuments of nature and 3 memorial monuments of nature, 9 strict natural reservations, 18 reservations for scientific research, 15 regions with special natural features, 25 characteristic landscapes, 17 special natural reservations, 150 distinctive vegetative kinds, 63 vegetative kinds in groups, 45 smaller groups, vegetative types in certain areas and 45 vegetative kinds cultivated in the urban and suburban areas, 247 animal kinds out of which 218 birds, 9 insects, 4 reptiles, 13 reptiles, 152 monuments of nature, out of which 24 geological and mineralogical- petro-graphic 19 geomorphologic, 77 hydro-graphic, 32 botanical, and 24 memorial.

Villagers in North Macedonia are known for tranquil atmosphere, and unique well-preserved crafts skills as woodcarving and filigree workshops and weaving *colorful traditional costumes*, rugs, blankets and carpets. In old bazaars (street markets) of North Macedonia in the larger cities, one comes across dozens of artisans which include small goldsmith and silversmith shops run by various local craftsmen and selling beautiful, delicate jewelry; *stomnari*, or urn-makers, who still produce glazed terracotta utensils such as urns, pitchers, cups, and bowls; and Asian-style carpet shops.

Though mostly mountainous, North Macedonia also encompassed the valleys of the Bistrica (Halijakmon), Vardar (Axios) and Struma rivers, all of which drain into the Aegean Sea. North Macedonia as also known as the *Vardar Macedonia* named after the Vardar River which flows almost the entire length of the country and makes its longest river. The spring of the Vardar river is one of the greatest natural beauties of the Gostivar region. There, near the Vrutok village, at an altitude of 683 meters, from the base of the mountain Sharr rises the Vardar river, and from the spring the riverbed widens. Vardar river passes through Gostivar, then the Derven canyon Skopje, Veles, Demir Kapija canyon, and crosses the Greek border near Gevgelija, Polykastro (Macedonian: Rugunovec) and Axioupoli ("town on the Axiós town of Vardar"), before flowing into the Aegean Sea in Central Macedonia west of Salonica (Macedonian: Thessaloniki Solun) in northern Greece (Aegean Macedonia).

In antiquity the area around the Erigon river present Crna Reka River or Black River, used to have name of Peonia with the first known capital of Bylazora or Vilazora, the present Veles. Strabo records the Erigon River which springs in the Illyrian mountains and flows through the areas of Lynkesta, Bryga, Deuriopa and Pelagona, to receives the tributaries of Osphagos and Bevus, and joins the Axios river by Stobi. The Illyrian tribe of Peones, recognized and recorded by Homer, settled possibly in this area which Strabo calls as *Amphaxitis*, that would literary mean our expression of *Povardarje*. Peones weiged war with the Pelagon tribe that originally lived in the area around the Crna Reka River, and Pelagon tribe settled in the southern area known as Pelagonia. The Vardar river valley has given its name to the *vardháris or vardarec*, a northerly prevailing ravine wind which blows down the length of the valley to bring cold conditions to the Thessaloniki area of Greece. Vardarec wind occurs when atmospheric pressure over eastern Europe is higher than over the Aegean Sea, as is often the case in winter or almost always in the Demir Kapija area.

For the local people of different parts of North Macedonia, waterfalls are places where religious holidays are traditionally celebrated, where illnesses are healed, where winter is bid farewell and spring welcome. Believed it or not, *there are about 150 waterfalls in North Macedonia* ! The highest one is on mountain Korab. It is 138 meters high and is located under the top of Mal Korab, near the former village Zuznje. Hidden in the deepest forests which cover 44% territory of North Macedonia, visited only by the bravest and the most persistent nature lovers, the North Macedonian waterfalls may provide an unique event and adventure. There are waterfalls on the mountains Korab, Shara, Jablanica, but the most visited are the waterfall in Smolare and Koleshino, at the gorgeous and steep slopes of the mountain Belasica. At the border between North Macedonia, Bulgaria and Greece, at 650 meters above the see level the Smolare waterfall is located. Smolare waterfall is one of the biggest waterfalls on Belasica Mountain, where the water falls from the rocks at a height of 35-40 meters. The area around the Smolare waterfall is abundant with vegetation and moss that never changes its green color. Here, during winter, nature creates the most beautiful icicles hanging over the rocks. In front of the Smolare waterfall there is a hole for which the locals tell their own story. The legend says that King Marko jumped with his horse from the waterfall, and the horse's shoe made a hole in the stone. The people from Smolare call this whole "dira". Combining these qualities with the country's dramatic mountains and canyons, its deep lakes and rivers, Macedonia has something for everyone...

Skopje is the capital of North Macedonia with over 600000 inhabitants. Major tourist centers of Macedonia are Ohrid, Struga, Prespa, Dojran and winter ski centers are Shar Planina Mountain, Pelister Mountain/National Park, Mavrovo Lake/National Park and Krushevo. The three ancient tectonic lakes of Ohrid, Prespa and Dojran have been protected by law, owing to their unique natural characteristics and their importance for science. Scenic Ohrid and Prespa Lakes are located close to each other and are surrounded by spectacular mountain ranges that provide abundance of natural and cultural attractions. In the gorgeous mountainous area above Ohrid and Struga are the municipalities of Debarca and *Vevcani* with some of the most interesting villages in the world. Every village has traditional architecture including churches, which are filled with burning candles, ancient murals and icons of Orthodox saints. There are picturesque stone houses and barns and outdoor ovens for baking bread and orchards and vineyards and fast flowing streams and old women dressed in colorful traditional costumes..... Here shepherds and their dogs tend flocks of sheep and goats and donkeys laden with hay nostalgically make their way down narrow trails and up cobblestone streets. In Vevcani village there is a complex of textile "washing mills", more than 300 years old, unique in the region and real rarity of Macedonia. All kinds of textile products are being washed and milled in these textile washing mills, but most of all the products such as bed covers, carpets, rugs etc are made of natural wool. When being dried on the pleasant Macedonia sun in the heart of the nature, they get beautiful. Every where there are friendly people eager to offer you priceless insights into their timeless existence...

Eastern part of North Macedonia is even more tempting. Forgotten by outsiders and North Macedonians alike, the enchanted east of the country is brimming over with natural beauty, historical attractions and sheer life. *"Poleka, poleka"* (*'slowly, slowly'*) say the North Macedonians; this approach to life helps explain a sluggish economy, but is also highly instructive for the way one should approach traveling in their country. A good time to go to the southeast of North Macedonia is the second week of September, when it's still hot but not oppressively so, and the red peppers are drying in every door frame, and the leaves are just starting to turn in the highest isolated peaks. Berovo sleepy village, 170 km from Skopje features a central position regarding the three airports in Skopje, Sofia and Thessaloniki. The villages around Berovo area flourish with time-honored tales of bleak nature and the hardy folk who've tamed it. In *Vladimirovo*, a few miles to the west of Berovo, locals speak reverentially of the man who wrestled a wolf with his bare hands until the beast was dead; no one can remember another case where such a thing was heard of. Berovo village is also well known for its potato and the white cheese. The Malesevo region is full of pine and oak trees, which is why Berovo craftsmen are well known for their skill in traditional wood crafting.

North Macedonia is of particular interest to visitors thanks to its *rare and exceptionally beautiful mountain landscape, rare flora and fauna, numerous cultural and historic sites, as well as traditional folklore.* Thanks to the relief characteristics, there are various climate types within the territory of North Macedonia, ranging from typically Mediterranean to typically continental climate. The specific topography and climate of North Macedonia and its varying hydrography have enabled the development of diverse flora and fauna. The mountains, national parks, protected areas and forests of Macedonia are renowned for their beauty and wilderness and is of great interest to tourists, offering the possibility to *organise various winter and outdoor sports*. According to the data of the State Statistical Office, the number of tourists in March 2014 was 36 290, and the number of nights spent by tourists was 78 721. The number of tourists in March 2014, compared to March 2013, increased by 5.2%, and the number of nights spent increased by 7.5%.

Major tourist centers/spots of Macedonia : Bitola, Dojran Lake, *Galicica National Park*, Jakupica Mountain, *Kokino Observatory*, Korab Mountain, Krusevo, Mariovo, Marko's Monastery, Matka Canyon, *Mavrovo Lake/National Park*, Ohrid, Ohrid Lake, *Pelister National Park,* Prespa Lake, Prilep, *Saint Panteleimon Monastery in Nerezi village, Saint John the Theologian Bigorski Monastery,* Scupi, Stobi, Struga, Skopje, Sar Mountain, Trebeniste village, Zrze Monastery....

Bargala Archaeological Site

Bargala was a Late Antiquity city first time mentioned in 451 AC on the surface of 5 hectares, near the present day town of Stip /10 km/, on the lower slopes of the Plachkovica Mountain. The name Bargala of the city which was of the Thracian origin has also been found on an inscription of the commemorative plaque from 371 on the city gates. Towards the end of the 4th century, the old settlement named Bargala served as a military camp of the Roman legions campaigning in the east. After demolition and citizens built a new city which developed into an important transport and trading center. The city of Bargala became an episcopal seat in the 5th and the 6th centuries, to have continued its importance and pinnacle during the Slavic era of rule. There were three basilica erected at the end of the 4th century and rebuilt and remodeled in the 5th and the 6th centuries.

The episcopal basilica in Bargala site which was built in the standard style of the Old Christian structures on the Balkan Peninsula and the Mediterranean was discovered in the northwest part of the city. It is three-aisle basilica with semi-circular inner and outer apses, with the inner narthex and an exonarthex. The stone plated basilica floors are particularly impressive, with the exception of the northern floor which is covered with a polychromatic mosaic and the ornament swastika. The structure of the Bargala basilica is rich in architectural decoration, of which are particularly interesting the marble capitals with lions heads and vine leaves and features the inscription discovered on a capital in the exo-narthex : *"Christ, help your servant, Bishop Hermius"*. The city of Bargala reached its pinnacle during the reign of Emperor Justinian I /527-565/. The mound with golden and bronze coins, latest dating from 584/5 was found at the Bargala site on the Bregalnica River. Among the most exclusive finds of Bargala site is a wood-carved plate dating from the end of the 4th century, the only one of its kind in the Balkans, which represents people and lions and geometric decorations.

In the close proximity of the Bargala site, outside the walls of the Early Christian town of Bargala, on the bank of the Kozjačka river, there is the Orthodox church dedicated to Saint George from the 9th-10th century, one of the oldest in Macedonia with fragments of fresco decoration that testify on rich cultural and spiritual life of the Slavic population of Stara Old Serbia.

Bitola

Bitola is a great ancient town in the south of the large fertile Pelagonija lowland, in southwestern Macedonia, some 14 km from the border between Greece and Macedonia, which represents an important junction between the Adriatic Sea, the Aegean Sea and the Central Europe. Bitola was called Monastir or Manastir in the past. Bitola is known as the *town of consuls*, since there were seven consulates in Bitola, as well as the important site on *the Via Egnatia, the former Roman trading route* that connected Thessaloniki with the Adriatic Sea.

Bitola has been established during the reign of the Macedonian King Samuil, eversince it bears the name derived from the Slavic word *"obitelj"* /family/ thanks to the large number of churches and monasteries. In the 10th century, Bitola was under the rule of the Bulgarian Tsar Samuil, but the Byzantine emperor Basil II recaptured Monastir (Bitola) in 1015. The town is mentioned as an episcopal center in 1019 in the record issued by Emperor Basil II. Two important uprisings against Byzantine rule took place in the Bitola area in 1040 and 1072. After the Bulgarian state was restored in the late 11th century, Bitola was incorporated under the rule of Tsar Kaloyan of Bulgaria. It was conquered again by Byzantium at the end of the 13th century, but it became part of Serbia in the first half of the 14th century, after the conquests of Stefan Dušan. From 1382 to 1912, Manastir was part of the Ottoman Empire. Fierce battles took place near the city during the arrival of Turkish forces. During the Ottoman rule the city of Bitola was the last capital of the Ottoman Rumelia. During the Ottoman era Bitola was the trade and administrative center with developed trade of wool, wheat, wax and leather. After the conquest of Macedonia by the Turks the native Serbian population went over to Mohammedanism to save their possessions, and their descendants are now followers of the Prophet.

During the Balkan War, According to the Treaty of Bucharest in 1913, the region of Macedonia was divided in 3 parts among Greeks, Serbs and Bulgarians. Bitola was to be in Bulgaria, according to a prewar alliance agreement between Bulgaria and Serbia, but the Serbian army entered the city and refused to hand it to Bulgaria. On the 19th November 1912 the regiment of the Drina division, Russian volunteers and Cossacks fulfilled the oath and marched into Bitolja which marked the end of the Bitola Battle. Previously they have liberated Kosovo and Metohija with the victory in the Kumanovo Battle, along with the 5th Regiment and other units of the Drina division of the Serbian Army and after several centuries they have fulfilled the *Kosovo oath*. During the First War World, Bitola was divided into French, Russian, Italian and Serbian regions, under the command of the French general Maurice Sarrail. Until Bulgaria's surrender in late autumn 1918, Bitola remained a front line city and was almost every day bombarded by airplanes and battery and suffered almost total destruction.

During the First WW Bitola was under the authority of the Central Powers and the Allied Powers. From autumn 1915 to autumn 1918 in the city passed numerous different armies (Bulgarian, German, French, Serbian, Russian, Italian), which were not always friendly behaved to the civilians. There was a lot of complaint about pillaging of property, especially in a time when there was no military action. Characteristic of the whole period of the war was the lack of basic foodstuffs, like flour, salt, petroleum, rice and so on. Bitola was turned into one of the largest medical military centers for the Serbian Army. The town of Bitola served as rescue of wounded Serbian solders, and from the middle of September to the end of December 1914 there arrived 4116 wounded soldiers, of which the largest number /3316/ arrived via Thessaloniki, while the rest arrived from Nis and Skopje. All the Serb solders were received in the Military hospital, and in its departments in the town. On the

Serb Military graveyard in Bitola, near the Heraclea site, there are 1321 crosses of the killed solders from Serbia during the First Balkan War and the First World War. The small metal crosses feature tricolors without any name of the fallen solder, but only a number....

The Thessaloniki Front /Macedonia Front/ broke-through in 15 September 1918. Bulgaria capitulated on 29th September 1918, while the Ottoman Empire capitulated on 30th October 1918. The Austria-Hungary Empire capitulated on 31st October 1918, and Germany capitulated on 11 December 1918. After the Kajmakchalan Battle, on the 19th of November 1916 the Serbian army liberated Bitola from Bulgarians, which was the first part of the Serbian lands liberated in the First WW. The Serbian Army was transferred in spring 1916 to the Thessaloniki Front which spread in several hundred kilometers, after it recovered from the Albania Golgotha on the Corfu island. Already in 1916 the Serb Army conquered the Kajmakchalan peak on the Nidze Mountain during the fierce battles face in face and large casualties in fights with Bulgarians. The real end of the First WW was on 28th June 1919, when the Versailles Peace Treaty was signed. After the military catastrophe in the First WW, the Austria-Hungary Empire was disbanded, and on its territory several successor states were created: Austria, Hungary, Czechoslovakia, Kingdom of Serbs, Croats and Slovenes, and Poland, and some its parts were added to Italy and Romania.

After the end of World War I (1918) Bitola was included in the Kingdom of Serbs, Croats and Slovenes, later called the Kingdom of Yugoslavia. During World War II (1941–1945), the Germans and later Bulgarians took control of the city. But in September 1944, Bulgaria switched sides in the war and withdrew from Yugoslavia, and Bitola was freed by Macedonian pro-Titoist Partisans. On 4 November, the 7th Macedonian Liberation Brigade entered Bitola victoriously. After the end of the war, a Macedonian state was established for the first time in modern history, within Yugoslavia.

Bitola is still rich in the numerous cultural monuments and various marks of its rich historical and cultural inheritance. The city of Bitola was known as "the City of Consuls" on account of the 12 diplomatic consuls who resided here from the time of the Berlin Congress of 1878 to 1913. When the Balkan wars terminated the Ottoman Empire and Bitola became part of the Kingdom of Yugoslavia, later constituent Republic of the Socialist Federative Republic of Yugoslavia. The old part of Bitola features well preserved architecture and bazaar-market and turn-of-the-century importance as a center for diplomacy within the Ottoman Empire while also exemplifies the country's time-honored cafe culture. The main street of Bitola Shirok Sokak dominates with its specific individualism, charm and beauty, featuring monumental urban folklore buildings, and colorful oriental and western European architecture, that is the most popular meeting point of both locals and visitors. Bitola and its surrounding are very rich in cultural and historical monuments that testify on the rich cultural and spiritual activity : The Clock Tower, Bezistan /covered oriental market/, Isak Chelebi Mosque, Ieni Mosque /present day Art Gallery/, Jewish Synagogue, the Church of "St. Dimitria", the Old Bazaar Stara carsija, the Prison-tower, St. Bogorodica Church... as well as delicious Turkish sweets lokum, produced under the traditional recipes and techniques.... Bitola is nicknamed "city of consuls" due to numerous colorful foreign consulates and is the second largest city in Macedonia with population of about 100000 inhabitants.

Dojran Lake

The Dojran Lake is the smallest tectonic lake of Macedonia, in East Macedonia, at the elevation of 148 meters, with the surface of 43,1 km2, of which 27,3 km2 belongs to Macedonia and 15,8 km2 to Greece. Dojran Lake is located in the ravine of the same name, at the south-easternmost part of Macedonia, spread between the Mountain of Belasica (2.036m) and its range of Bosak in the north, and the Kruša Planina Mt (1.179m) and Karadag Mt in the east, and the shallow Trnovo Planina Mt, or the Kara Bali, to the west and southwest. To the south, the ravine of Dojran spreads direction the Kukus area, and further to the Salonica Bay Thessaloniki Bay in Greece. Dojran Lake is only 25 km away from the E-75 Highway, 80 km from Salonica /Thessaloniki/ and 166 km from Macedonian capital Skopje.

Dojran lake features shape similar to a circle and it is 9 km long and 7 km wide. 15 types of fish of special features are found in Dojran Lake /of which famous are *kostreš, plašica, carp, sheath-fish*/ and water grass /*algae*/. All those fish species contributed t the fame of the Dojran Lake as part of the world's natural rarities. Dojran Lake is *the richest lake in fish in Europe* and very rich in vegetation. The /notorious/ Dojran Lake fishermen still fish during winter period in a very special ancient way of fishing with the assistance of birds /Cormorants and other diving birds/. The climate in the Dojran plain is pleasant moderate Mediterranean as the entire Dojran Lake region is under the climatic influence of the Salonica gulf. The climate of Dojran Lake is characterized with warm and dry summers and soft winters. In Dojran Lake over 120 days during the year feature temperature over 26°C.

The settlement on the present day Stari Dojran existed in the prehistory and Greek historian Heredotus in the 5th century BC mentions the Paeonians, ancient Thraco-Illyrian tribe which settled the territory. During the rule of Philip II (359-336) and Alexander The Great (336-323) of Macedonia and during the Roman conquest and occupation of the Balkans in the 2nd century BC, there was the antique city covering some 30 hectares a fort with the oldest known name being Taurian. In 395 the city became part of the Eastern Roman Empire Roumelia, later called the Byzantine Empire. Around the 6th 7th century the Slavic tribes settle the Balkans and the city of Taurian, thanks to its location and the development, takes a big part in the historical, cultural and economical issues.

The city of Polin which was slightly relocated to the south inherits the tradition of Taurian and the main developments were with fishing, hunting and farming. However being at the crossroads of the conquering campaigns of the Byzantines and the Macedonian empire of Tzar Samuil (around 969-1018 AD) also a path for the Serbian conquerors King Milutin 1281 and Tzar Dushan 1331-1355 AD, the city experienced some unpleasant times after which arrived Turks of the Ottoman Empire who gave the city the name Dojran. The city was rebuilt along the similar architecture as Constantinople and Thessaloniki, with cobblestone streets, fresh water fountains, city bath, churches and also mosques, several schools, a clock tower etc. The area of Dojran at that time assumed to have had 79 villages with about 30000 residents.

Unfortunately World War I brought an end to the prosperous life of Dojran for a while. In 1916 the entire population of Dojran was terrified and evacuated to neighboring towns and countries and in 1918 completely moved due to harsh military actions and bombardment in the vicinity when Dojran was completely destroyed. The old residents however had plans to rebuild the city in the period between the two Great wars, but several obstacles stood in the way, one of which was the lake and the flooding of the demolished city. Having the urge to return to their ancestral homes about 60 fishermen families, around 1919-1920 decided to reside at the foundation of the old city of Taurian. So, 4 km from the ruins of Dojran they create a new settlement and call it Nov (New) Dojran.

As time went on many of the families returned to the old Dojran as well. The administrative buildings were built in Old Dojran so both settlements started developing simultaneously. In World War II the city was a victim of foreign conquests once more until the final liberation on November 5th 1944, when it was included in the Peoples Republic of Macedonia as part of Yugoslavia and since 1991 is a part of independent Republic of Macedonia.

Galičica National Park

The slopes of fantastic Galichica National Park, a spectacular mountain range rises to 2254 meters between Ohrid Lake to the west and Prespa Lake to the east. These stunning lakes are set high in the Galicica mountain range, created by tectonic shifts in the Paleozoic period cca 300 millions years ago, with Prespa Lake at 850 meters and Ohrid Lake at 693 meters, covering an area of 22750 hectares of gorgeous nature. Galichica Mountain was declared the National Park in 1958 and encompasses area of the shores of both Prespa lakes as well as the island of *Golem Grad* in the Prespa Lake, which is rocky unpopulated island, known as the island of snakes, as there is huge habitat of those vertebrates. The highest point of Galičica National Park is the *summit Magaro* 2255 meters above sea level while the south border of the National Park is also a national border with *Republic of Albania.* On the north, the Galičica National Park border line passes through several landmarks, and connects both lakes making scenery of incomparable beauty.

130 different forest communities have been discovered within the Galičica National Park what indicated that the vegetation in the Galichica National Park is very rich, including extremely rare floral types. Particularly distinctive are the relief characteristics of the Galicica region : the high mountain peaks that exceed 2000 meters, the forested area, and in the higher areas, the vast pastures with

plenty of various medicinal herbs which decorate the mountain scenery. Well marked mountaineering and hiking trails and rich cultural inheritance of the Galičica National Park and surroundings attract nature and culture lovers. The lower slopes of Galicica Mountain reach the edge of the both wonderful lakes and provide views of extraordinary and unforgettable beauty.

Heraclea Lyncestis Archaeological Site

Famous for its dazzling mosaics, impressive ancient theater and Roman baths, Heraclea Lynkestis is the most vividly preserved city from the Ancient Macedonian Empire named after the Greek hero Heracles. It is believed that Heraclea was founded in the 4th century B.C. by the Philip of Macedonia and conquered by the Romans two centuries later /in 168 B.C./. Heraclea Lynkestis was built in the vast fertile Pelagonia plain and on the *Via Egnatia* road and became one of the key stations on this trading route. From the 4th-6th centuries A.D. Heraclea Lynkestis also was an Episcopal seat.

The first excavations in Heraclea Lynkestis were carried out before the First World War, but only since then have the full glories of the ancient city been revealed. The architectonic remains and the imposing number of movable finds of 2300 inventoried objects and the numerous deposited materials of the Heraclea site are a strong confirmation of the continuous life of this wonderful ancient Macedonian town between the 4th century BC and the 11th century AD. Beautiful Roman baths, the Episcopal church, three-nave Basilica and baptistery, wonderful statue of Hercules, money minted by glorious kings and rules /among them Alexander the Great/, a Jewish temple, portico and a Roman theater wonderfully decorated by rich floor mosaics. Heraclea mosaics are considered the best preserved and artistically most valuable works of that period not only in Macedonia, but in the world. Heraclea Lynkestis hoards and treasury make highlights of Macedonia, and its remains which survive in excellent conditions are present day used for summer concerts and theater shows. Heraclea Lynkestis archaeological site is 2,5 km away from center of Bitola, in central Macedonia.

Jakupica Mountain

Jakupica is a mountain range in the central part of the Republic of Macedonia. The highest peak of Jakupica Mountain is the Solunska Glava peak /2540 meters above the sea level/ named after the majestic view that spreads towards Thessaloniki and the Aegean Sea in clear calm days. Other significant peaks of Jakupica Mountain are: Karadzica /2,473 m/, Popovo Brdo /2,380 m/, Ostar Breg /2,365 m/, Ubava /2,353 m/, Ostar Vrv /2,275 m/, and Dautica /2,178 m/. Jakupica Mountain is not a natural park, but it is very rich in woods and wild life as well. The most attractive part of the Jakupica Mountain is its southern part, where one of the wonders of nature Rock, 700 meters high and 1,5 km wide is located. The name of this rock is Nezilovska Stena. Springs of Babuna River are located in the foothill of Nezilovska Stena.

The terrain of Jakupica Mountain is crisscrossed by numerous clear and fast mountain rivers. Large areasof Jakupica Mountain are covered with beech, oak, and conifer forests. There are also obvious traces of the primeval glaciation from the dilluvial period. A number of liable institutions have been recommending the promotion of this area /and the one of the Sar Mountains/ into a national park. The mountain range of Jakupica can be easily approached from the capital Skopje, or from the town of Veles and many villages in the area.

David Thompson

Kokino Megalithic Observatory

Kokino is an important ancient archaeological site, a prehistorical sanctuary and a megalithic observatory in the northeastern Republic of Macedonia, about 35 km from the town of Kumanovo, near the villages of Staro Nagoricane and Kokino. Kokino was discovered in 2001 by archaeologist Jovica Stankovski and was named by the nearby village of Kokino. Kokino site is situated 1030 m above sea level on the Tatićev Kamen Summit andesite rocks of an unusual shape and covers an area of a 100-meter radius. Historical and archaeological data of the River Pchinja valley as a natural corridor located in the central part of the Balkan Peninsula are recording the great importance of the river valley in the times of constant movement of the people as well as war expeditions that were passing in the north-south direction.

The Kokino site is more than 3800 years old. Kokino sanctuary megalithic observatory consists of two parts. The oldest archaeological finds from Kokino site date from the Iron Period, around the 7th century BC. Finds from the Middle Bronze Age are the most numerous /mainly ceramic vessels, stone-mills and a few molds/. An agglomeration from the Iron Age has also been discovered at the Kokino sanctuary. Several stone seats (thrones) are dominant on the Kokino site and they are pointing towards the east horizon. They include special stone markers used to track the movement of the Sun and Moon on the eastern horizon. It was discovered that the Kokino site, in the course of the whole second millennium B.C. was used both as an Observatory and the sanctuary, which indicates a high level of cultural progress and social organization of inhabitants who used the observatory. Analysis showed that days when special rituals were held, especially those of the harvest were marked on a most appropriate way. The end of July is time when the harvest is completed, thus this ritual was linked to the glorification of this activity. According to the believes of the people of that time, in the moment when the tribe leader was enlightened ritually he unified with the God Sun and that was a assurance that next year would bring rich harvest, good and peaceful life. In the course of one calendar year, Sun and the Full Moon rise in different places on horizon, also determining the so called extreme rise positions on the horizon. This mean that Sun in winter when the day is the shortest or in the day of the winter solstice /22nd of December/ rises in it's the southernmost position on the horizon. Then, day by day it moves towards the north and on the day of vernal equinox / 21st of March/ Sun rises on east. Sun continues to move toward the north, the length of the day increases and in the day of summer solstice /21st of June/ Sun reaches its northernmost point on the horizon. After that Sun returns back and in a day of the autumn equinox /23rd of September/ again it will rise on east, and on 22nd of December it will complete the cycle rising in the winter solstice point. Evidence for this can be found in huge number of archaeological findings of terracotta, especially large number of manual mils for grain.

A Kokino culture may have been found, after a network of 10 temples were discovered in the mountain peaks of the Kumanovo-Kratovo-Zletovo volcanic region, dating back to the 20th-18th century BC. Stone drawings have also been discovered at the Kokino site, especially those of the eagle (associated with storms), and turtles (symbol of country). At least ten figurine objects of humans and animals have been discovered. If Kokino is identified as an ancient civilization, it would be the oldest known in the Balkans. The Kokino prehistorical sanctuary site megalithic observatory was recognized by the United States Space Agency (NASA) as a significant heritage site of this type in its "Timeless knowledge" project in 2005. It listed Kokino side by side with ancient observatories as Stonehenge in Great Britain, Abu Simbel in Egypt and Angkor Wat in Cambodia. Kokino site megalithic observatory has been nominated to be included on UNESCO World Heritage list.

Korab Mountain

Mount Korab /"Golem Korab") is the highest mountain of both Albania and Macedonia. Actually, the Korab's gigantic peaks form a frontier between the two Balkan countries. The Korab mountain is adjacent to the Sar Mountains /Sharr Mountain/ and makes the most stunning and the most beautiful mountainous terrain of Macedonia which is part of the Mavrovo National Park. The Korab Mountain features a number of gigantic peaks that are higher than 2000 meters and its range stretches over 40 kilometers in a north-south direction between the lower section of the Black Drin River and its tributary Radika River.

Small Korab Gate is the mountain pass on the border of Albania and the Republic of Macedonia situated southwest of the main Korab Mountain summit, which is the highest mountain of both countries. Small Korab Gate is high, and is 403 m higher than the Big Korab Gate on the northern slope of Mount Korab. The state border intersects the higher peak, Great Korab. Ascent from the Republic of Macedonian side involves entering the Republic of Macedonian-Albanian boundary area, for which a special permit is required from the Ministry of Internal Affairs of the Republic of Macedonia. There are many routes up to Korab Mt, though the mountains is mostly climbed from the Macedonian side, which has more organized hiking and mountaineering activities than Albania presently has. The Korab Mountain is home to the spectacular Korab waterfall in the upper valley of the Dlaboka reka river. During spring time, the waterfall reaches height of over 130 meters, which makes it the highest waterfall in Macedonia.

These Korab Mt peaks are occasionally ruptured by radial tectonics in the shape of blocks that end in the valley of the Radika river on the Macedonian side of steep slopes. Particularly remarkable is also the alpine area of Kabaš with several sheer and hardly approachable peaks. In its highest part, the climate is alpine and includes some alpine flora elements. The magic of Korab Mountain is even more alluring thanks to 8 beautiful glacial lakes. The largest lake on Mount Korab is Grame Lake located on the Mali i Grames in Albania. The Korab mountain sides are frequently covered with snow throughout the year, so that some of them are perfectly attractive and suitable for winter sports. Deciduous and evergreen trees, spacious pastures, green meadows and other vegetation, can be found along the Korab mountain. Korab Mountain is a traditional area for sheep breeding and is considered to be one of the largest pasture areas of Europe. Korab Mountain contains numerous natural monuments such as glacial lakes, glacial caves and spectacular canyons.

Kratovo

Kratovo is small, beautiful, sleepy picturesque town in north-east Macedonia, with population of nearly 7000, around 80 km east of Skopje, on both banks of the Kratovo River. Kratovo is significantly distinctive in its rich cultural heritage, history and tradition, numerous arched stone bridges, original Medieval Balkan architecture with authentic historical trade quarter *charshi,* number of multi storey stone towers of thick walls, attractive crafts workshops and tiny traditional shops, small cafes and restaurants, curvy narrow cobblestone streets, lush mountain pastures, fresh mountainous air and outstandingly welcoming and friendly local people. In the close vicinity of Kratovo there is wealth of natural and cultural sites to discover and see the Kuklica locality */unique row of high stone formations/, Saint George Monastery Staro*

Nagoricane, Saint John of Osogovo Monastery, Saint Nicholas Psaca Monastery, Lesnovo Monastery.... The nearby /15 km/ Stone Town of Kuklica is famous for its 10 million years old 120 stone figures "stone dolls", reaching heights of 10 meters. Kuklica means doll in Macedonian, thus comes the name of the site and the village.

Kratovo is historical municipality in the north-eastern part of Macedonia which borders with *Staro Nagoricane* and *Kriva Palanka* Municipalities in the north, and Kocani Municipality in the east, and Kumanovo in the west and Probistip in the south. Kratovo is set on the western slopes of *Osogovo Mountain*, on both sides of the Kratovska River, *at the bottom of an extinct volcanic crater*, at an altitude of some 700 meters. Kratovo Municipality covers an area of 220 ha and features a moderate continental climate with an average annual air temperature of 11,6°C and the average amount of rainfall of 700 mm. Kratovo is considered one of the oldest urban settlements in the Balkans. Legend has it that the town got its name of Kratovo because of the place similar to crater where it has been built upon.

Under the name *of Cratiscara* is was mentioned in Roman time and under the name of *Koritos* during Byzantium. The trade of handmade gold, silver and copper items and objects was particularly developed of that time. In the Middle Ages Kratovo was an important mining and commercial center of the "golden era" of the Serbian state, ruled by the Nemanjic dynasty and successors. People from Dubrovnik had their significant trading colony here. Apart from the predominanlty Serb local population of Kratovo and tradesman from Dubrovnik, there were also settled Saxons miners who have dealt with mining, crafts, construction, filigree who received lead, zinc, silver, gold, copper and iron from rich Kratovo mines. In 1282 Kratovo had become an important mining center, thanks to the experienced miners Saxons who came to activate the mines. During the reign of Tsar Dusan, Kratovo mines were the main source of wealth of the local ruler Jovan Oliver. Later was Kratovo inherited by Dragas and Kostadin Dejanovic, with whom Dubrovnik traders kept friendly relationship. Since its foundation most probablyin the last decade of the 15th century, the Kratovo mint was the second biggest producer in the Ottoman Empire, after Novo Brdo, that continued through an during the first six decades of the 16th century.

The noble families of Pepic and Bojkic lived in Kratovo in the 15th century and were engaged in mining and goldsmiths for which they received special recognition and support from the Turks. The monastic novice Dmitar in 1466 copied the *Nomocanon of Saint Sava* Book /the highest code in the Serbian Orthodox Church, finished in 1219/ for needs of the Ohrid archbishops Doroteus and Mark as such book did not exist. The importance of that place can be judged through the visit of Sultan Murat who was moving with his army towards Kosovo, but stayed there in order to visit the the town, already renown of gold and silver. The intense mining continued during the Turkish rule and in the 16th and here during the 18th century silver coins were minted. Besides prosperity and financial aspect, special attention was given to the mint employees who mostly lived in the *mahala of goldsmiths and in the mahala of mint*, during the reign of sultan Suleiman the Magnificent.

After the Austrian-Turkish War of 1689 to 1690 and the Karposh uprising, the city was destroyed, and mine shafts closed. The Austrian-Turkish war was result of the expansionist policy of the Ottoman Empire which wanted to gain its imperial aims in constant extension of its borders. The mining exploitation continued, until the Karpos Uprising in 1689, when the town was devastated and the mine closed. The Turks were forced to retreat, after their defeat by the Austrian-Polish troops in Vienna in 1683. This catastrophic and unprecedented defeat resulted in various risings in the conquered southern parts of the Balkan Peninsula, as the Hapsburg rulers enhanced Christian population to rebel and fight against the Ottomans.

While the Austrians were spreading towards the Turkish regions in Serbia and getting more deeply in Turkey, in Macedonia by the way, there were the aggressive units of the local movement for liberation, that was becoming an local uprising. That uprising in the history sources, is known as the Karpos uprising. The life of the miners of the Kratovo basin was unbearable. Exploitation reached a climax and the miners rose under the leadership of the Karpos, a peasant miner and also the hajduk (high-duke, outlaw). They liberated the fortified Kratovo and Kriva Palanka and came far as Veles and Demir Kapija (Iron Door). This is a reason that the Turkish Sultan sent message to the Grand Vizier's of Nis, Leskovac, and Vranje to attack this "outlaw formations". He even mentioned that he wants Karpos to be punished in every possible way. Karpos was already a leader to 15,000 up-risers, and tried to take over the control of Skopje, with support of the Austrian army. Then, the Austrians appeared outside Skopje but were driven away by the Turks who, during that time, were defeated on several occasions by the Austrians. The Austrian general Picolomini led his army through Kosovo (then a Turkish province) and Kachanik Gorge and penetrated as far as Skopje. The Austrians defeated the Turkish troops and with the help of the Karposh rebels entered Skopje which had already been liberated. Picolomini arrived in Skopje on October 25th, 1689.

He didn't intend to go south, but through Albania direction Durres, wishing to destroy the Turkish fortification and thus to fill the Turks with terror. But unfortunately, there was a plague epidemics spread everywhere. The next day on October 26th, the *general Picolomini* commanded his soldiers to set fire in Skopje, and like Nero he watched the fire while listening to the music of his military band. He wrote all this to his King Leopold 1st. After the fire, the Austrian army withdrew to Kachanik Pass and Kosovo. But the general Picolomini, had been infected by the plague in Skopje, and he died in the morning of November 9th. The general forces of the uprising were settled in the liberated towns of Kriva Palanka and Kumanovo. After the massive attacks of the Turkish-Tatar troops this cities fall gain under Turkish rule. The Turks gathered their army and the staff held a counsel at Edrine, where the question of overcoming the uprising of the Macedonian miners under the leadership of Karpos was discussed.

The task was carried out by Halil Pasha, who retook all the places that have been liberated by the miners. Skopje was the last to surrender. Karpos was captured in Kumanovo and brought to Skopje, where he was hung on a tree near the Stone Bridge, butchered by soldiers and thrown into the muddy waters of the Vardar river. This was the bloody and the tragic end of the Karpos uprising, at the beginning of December 1689. In 1805 the mine was rented by Ali-Beg Majdemdzija and the work continued. According to the manuscripts of Amu Bue, that town had in 1836 56,000 inhabitants. Until the end of the 19th century the town of Kratovo rapidly stagnated and the once most beautiful "Carsija" with goldsmith's and silversmith's shops decayed. In the beginning of the 19th century center of mining becomes Zletovo while in Kratovo completely ceases mining activity. At the end of the 19th century in Kratovo lived 4,500 residents of whom a significant number were Turks. Since 1912 large part of Turks had moved and Kratovo turned into a small urban settlement and in 1931 it had only 1.883 inhabitants.

Kratovo is the seat of Kratovo Municipality, which covers an area of 37,544 ha, has 31 township with 10,441 inhabitants. The Kratovo population is mainly employed in the mining industry. There is a non-metallic mine, factory Bruce, plastic and textile factory and excellent conditions for tourism. Kratovo features well preserved stone houses with red roofs erected in old town architecture, attractive *arched stone bridges,* among the most prominent being *Radin, Johchiski and Charsiski (bazaar) Bridge* and medieval towers of which 3 are famous the Simikjevata, Haji Kostovata and Emin Bey Tower. The Kratovo Clock Tower /built in 1372/ is one of the six towers that survived from the medieval and the Turkish period of history. On the third floor visitors can relax, looking through some of the windows or balcony to the medieval Kratovo....

Dordje of Kratovo was Serb, born in the 16th century by prominent Christians Dimitrije and Sara. As Djordje's father dies early his mother sents Djordje to town of Serdica the present Sofia to learn craftsmanship of goldsmiths and silversmiths. Being goldsmith in the Middle ages provided a highly reputation in exclusively urban society with large fines enacted by the Tsar Dusan Code for goldsmiths who did not obey and remained to live in villages. In Sofia young Djordje started to get goldsmiths skills, but also learned and read liturgical books of his Orthodox faith. Djordje regularly attended the liturgies and had excellent teacher and spiritual father, highly educated priest Peter, better known as Pop Peja. Contrary to the Christian calmness, during the reign of sultan Selim, young Djordje came into disagreement with powerful ulemas and hodzas of the Sofia sanjak when he refused to convert to Islam with offered option to gain higher social status and honor, and opportunity to become more urban and richer.

As victim of slander that he had profaned Mohammedan religion and blasphemed Mohammed, Djordje was taken to prison and after torture exposed to the judges who blackmailed him with proposition either to convert or to be executed in public in bonfire. That is how young Djordje brutally ended in Sofia, burned alive at the stake being only 18 years old. Several months later the holy remains of Djordje Kratovac /of Kratovo/ were dig out and placed in a coffin in the Church of Saint John Chrysostom in Kratovo.

Respecting the memory of Djordje Kratovac, the goldsmiths of Sofia proclaimed the day when Djordje died, 11th of February 1515 for their patron day /protector of goldsmiths/. The earliest hagiography of the Holy New martyr George of Kratovo dates from the 17th century, as the manuscript 479 from the Hilandar Monastery, as well as the Serbian-Slavic manuscript which was originally kept in the Rila Monastery and now is exposed in the *National Library in Sofia*. When Pajsije bishop of Hilandar Monastery went in 1550 to visit the Tsar Ivan Vasilyevich Grozny Ivan *the Terrible, he gifted the tsar with the double-sided icon bearing depictions of the King Milutin and King Stefan of Decani on one side, and depictions of the Holy Prince Lazar and Holy Martyr George of Kratovo on the other side.*

This Orthodox martyr is depicted in many Serbian monasteries and churches and his cult was widely spread and respected. In 1925 a church dedicated to this Orthodox Christian martyr was built in the center of Kratovo, with the monument erected to this *martyr the saint of Kratovo*. The particle of the holy relics of Saint George martyr of Kratovo is kept in the festive ornate coffin /gifted by the Union of goldsmiths of Serbia/, in the monastic church of the Shroud of the Holy Virgin in Mala Remeta Monastery on southern slopes of Fruska Gora Mountain. The Mala Remeta Monastery celebrates its feast of the Shroud of the Holy Virgin on 14 October, but also celebrates the Saint George, Newmartyr of Kratovo on the 24 February.

Krushevo Kruševo

Kruševo is a picturesque mountainous town in Central-south Macedonia, on the slopes of the Busava mountain, making the *highest town in Macedonia*, surrounded with impeccable eco environment. Krusevo is situated at the altitude of 1350 meters, right above the north-western part of Pelagonija plain that stretches south to the Greek border. Krusevo has around 5000 inhabitants. Krushevo is one of the *highest cities in the Balkans,* located 160 km from the capital Skopje, 55 km from Bitola, 32 km from Prilep, and only 70 km from the Macedonian Greek crossing border "Medzitlia Niki". The town of Krusevo is adorned with old nicely refurbished and more recent original houses built in the style of old Macedonian architecture /white facades and red roofs/ leaving the town with virtually no apartment blocks.

Kruševo can be accessed by good paved road from Prilep that is 32 km away, passing along scenic landscapes. Situated at an altitude of 1,350 meters, Kruševo is the highest town in the Republic of Macedonia, and one of the highest settlements in the Balkans, entirely surrounded with magnificent fresh air, thick beech and pine forests, slopes and fields that are outstanding for winter sports and various outdoor activities, among which flying paragliding is world famous and best place for paragliding. Paraglider's comment *'Simply the best site to practice thermal flying. It's not easy to fly there but if one can master flying in Krusevo, one can fly anywhere'.*

Kruševo is known for its many fine houses examples of the 19th century traditional architecture, plenty of small cafes and traditional restaurants. The town of Kruševo is full of old and more recent houses built in the style of the old original Aromanian /Vlach-Wallachian/ architecture. The town of Krusevo was founded by Macedonians in the 15th century. Kruševo experienced its cultural and economic growth and pinnacle when Aromunians from Epirus, in particular from Moscopolis, settled there in the the 18th century. Today we have in Krusevo the highest concentration of Aromanians-Armans in Macedonia. The Kruševo towns galleries include a wonderful collections and exhibits of the 19th century icons and a memorial to the master of modern Aromanian painting

Nikola Martinovski who was born in this town. Krusevo has a number of museums of the Ilinden Uprising.

The city of Krusevo is the most famous center of the rebellion liberation struggle and revolutionary movement against the Ottoman Empire, holding an important place in the country's historical identity. All started on the 2nd August 1903 by freeing the Macedonian mountain town of Kruševo from the Ottoman Empire and resulted in the creation of the first free Republic of the Balkans, called the Krusevo Republic, declared as an independent state. After ten days, the Ottomans sent an overwhelming force into the Krusevo hills and crushed the uprising. Many of the Krusevo rebellions had been killed and-or went through traumatic experiences, in many cases had suddenly lost their families, friends and property, of whom Pitu Guli was perhaps the best known. Many more had gone into exile in Bulgaria, among them Nikola Karev. Krusevo is home to the Mečkin Kamen historical landmark which marks the spot of the Ilinden uprising of 1903, celebrating the only independent area in the whole of the Ottoman Republic at the time. On the 2nd of August every year, the Meckin Kamen is the site of the traditional celebrations of the Macedonian Independence Day. Kruševo also hosts the impressive Makedonium monument dedicated to the Ilinden Uprising and to local partisan battles in 1941-44, designed by Iskra Grabuloska and Jordan Grabuloski in 1974. The Ilinden Memorial or 'Makedonium' at Kruševo commemorates the resistance fighters who took part in the Ilinden Uprising of 1903 against the Ottoman Empire, while also remembering the Partisan fighters of National Liberation War (WWII).

Krusevo is hometown of *Todor Toše Proeski* /January 25, 1981 October 16, 2007/. Toše Proeski was the young Macedonian multi-genre talented singer, songwriter and actor. His successful career began in 1996 when he participated in the teenage music festival

Melfest in Prilep. Toše Proeski was popular across the entire Balkan area and further north, and locally he was considered a top act of the Macedonian music scene. Proeski was known for his strong vocal performances and trademark of "Ve sakam site" /I Love You All/. His most famous songs are : "Solzi Pravat Zlaten Prsten" ("Tears Make a Golden Ring"), Sinot Božji (The Son of God), "Izlaži me Ušte Ednaš" ("Lie to Me One More Time"), "Vo Kosi da ti Spijam" ("Sleeping in Your Hair"), "Iluzija" ("Illusion") "Tajno Moja" ("Secret of Mine"), "Ako me Pogledneš vo Oči" ("If You Look Into My Eyes"), "Čija Si" ("To Whom Do You Belong?"), "Malečka" ("Little One") and "Polsko Cvece" ("Field Flower"), "Igri Bez Granici" ("Game Without Borders"), "Najteza stvar" ("The hardest Thing"). Toše was awarded with the Mother Theresa Humanitarian Award and in 2003 he became a Regional UNICEF Ambassador. Toše died in a tragic car crash on 16th of October 2007. October 17 was pronounced a national day of mourning in Macedonia. The three days following his death were pronounced days of mourning in the City of Kruševo. Spontaneous mourning of thousands of people lighting candles in memory of Toše Proeski gathered throughout the Balkans. The government of the Republic of Macedonia gave him the title "Honorable citizen of Macedonia". The Memorial Museum of Toše Proeski in Kruševo houses all possessions from Toše' life his toys, sports equipment, guitars, clothing. Tose's songs are played throughout the glass windows of the memorial house. Nearby is the grave of Tose Proeski, covered by numerous flowers and gifts left by fans that miss him and remember him.

Thanks to its elevation, Kruševo is one of Macedonia's winter sports destinations and surely features the perfect world known paragliding conditions; the same quality also makes this pine-forested getaway a comfortable destination in summer, when the Kruševo air stays cooler and more pure than in the arid lowlands.

Kumanovo Zebrnjak Memorial

The Zebrnjak is memorial monument dedicated to the heroic fallen soldiers of the Kumanovo Battle the major Battle of the First Balkan War, which symbolizes heroic Serbian sacrifices and victims fall for freedom which marked beginning of the liberation of the *Stara Srbija Old Serbia and Macedonia from the Turkish rule.* Zebrnjak Monument is located on 511 meters hill in the center of the vast Kumanovo plain, at the edge of Mlado Nagoricane village, 6 km away from town of Kumanovo, in then Vardar Banovina the province of then Kingdom of Yugoslavia, today in present North Macedonia. The Zebrnjak Monument with the ossuary has been erected in 1937 for the 25th anniversary of the Kumanovo Battle which took place on the 23rd and the 24th October 1912 during the First Balkan War, between the Turkish Vardar Army and the First Serbian Army.

Superintendent of the Supreme Command and the Serbian Commander in Chief of the Kumanovo Battle was *Radomir Putnik* and his deputy was general *Živojin Mišic*. The objective of the Serbian army plan was to destroy the Ottoman army in a decisive battle before the Ottomans could complete the mobilization and concentration of forces. The Serbian planners assumed that the main Ottoman force would be deployed defensively in the valley of Vardar River and on the strategically important plateau of Ovce Pole. The strategic plan of the Serbian Supreme Command planned that the First army, led by the regent Aleksandar Karadjorđević, whose right wing was settled at the edges of the Skopska Crna Gora Mt and the left wing was in the Pčinja river valley, advance through Kumanovo with the aim to defeat and deter the enemy at the decisive Ovce Polje battle. The aim was to double envelop the Ottoman army by using three armies: First army under Crown Prince Alexander, comprising five infantry and one cavalry division (132,000 men), was deployed in the area around Vranje, with the task to attack the enemy frontally. Second army under Stepa Stepanovic, comprising one Serbian and one Bulgarian division (74,000 men), deployed in the area around Kyustendil, was assigned to the easternmost attack, with the objective of attacking the right flank of the enemy. Third Army, under Bozidar Jankovic, comprising four infantry divisions and one infantry brigade (76,000 men), deployed in two groups, the first one at Toplica and the second one at Medvedja, was assigned to the westernmost attack, with the task to take Kosovo and then move south to attack the left flank of the enemy.

According to the initial Ottoman plan created by Colmar Freiherr von der Goltz, the Ottoman forces in Macedonia would stay in defense and, if necessary, retreat to Albania. The decisive battle would take place in Thrace, versus the Bulgarian army. However, Nazim Pasha, the newly appointed commander-in-chief of the Ottoman army, decided to surprise the Serbs by taking an offense in Macedonia. The plan also included the offense in Thrace. His goal was to win the initial battles against the surprised allies, hoping that the Great powers would then intervene and stop the war. But the first and biggest mistake was Nazim Pasha's decision to immediately bring the fight to the invading armies, which resulted in disaster when ill-prepared and only partially mobilized Turkish forces confronted the Serbs at Kumanovo on October 23 and 24, and the Bulgarians in the simultaneous battle of Kirk Kilisse, October 22-24. The Ottoman mobilization in Macedonia was slow, and the Ottoman Vardar Army, led by Zeki Pasha, had little more than a half of its manpower mobilized when the war started. The army comprised of the Fifth Corps, under Said Pasha, comprising 4 divisions /32000 men/, deployed in the area around Stip, Sixth Corps under Cavit Pasha, comprising two divisions /6000 men/, deployed in the area around Veles, and the Seventh Corps, under

Fethi Pasha, comprising three divisions /19000 men/, deployed in the area around Kumanovo and smaller units in Kosovo area.

The morning of 23 October 1912 was foggy and reconnaissance could not be performed properly. On the Serbian left flank, the observers noticed the troops of the 17th Infantry Division in movement, but mistook them for the Ottoman battery withdrawing from Stracin. Troops of the 18th regiment of Danube Division I, which moved forward to capture it, were pushed back, as well as the reconnaissance forces of Cavalry Division. Observing the retreat of these Serbian units, Zeki Pasha concluded that the Serbian left wing was weak. Since there were no actions of the Second Army from Stracin, he decided to attack. Around 11:00, with artillery support, 5th and the 6th Corps attacked the positions of the Danube Division I. Soon, 13th and 17th Infantry Division forced the 18th regiment to retreat in disorder, but, instead of continuing the attack, Zeki Pasha waited for the arrival of Štip Infantry Division from the rear to use this division for attack on the Serbian flank and rear.

That enabled the Serbian 7th regiment to aid the wavering 18th regiment and to consolidate a defense. Soon after that, the Serbian 8th regiment arrived, and the 7th regiment was able to move to the left flank and reinforce the defense of Srtevica, which was endangered by an attack of Štip Infantry Division. On the right flank of Danube Division I, its 9th regiment halted the advance of the weakened Monastir Bitola Infantry Division. Around 12:00, the 7th Corps started its attack on the positions held by Morava Division I. However, Serbian infantry and artillery were already deployed for combat, as the artillery fire from the east suggested that the battle has started. After the initial Ottoman progress, Serbs counterattacked and pushed them back to their starting positions. After the Serbian counterattack, Ottoman units were kept at bay by the well organized Serbian artillery fire until the end of day. The

Serbian rear echelon divisions (Danube Division II on the left, Drina Division I in the center and Timok Division II on the right) and the army artillery were not informed about the combat operations. They remained in the rear, without participating in the first day of the Kumanovo battle. The First Army command did not receive precise information about the battle and did not have any influence on the actual combat. Despite these facts, the Ottoman attack of the 23 October was not successful, mostly thanks to "the high devotion of (Serbian) troops and lower officers".

Uninformed about the situation in the field, the Serbian First Army command did not realize that the attack of the main Ottoman forces had occurred, as those forces were expected on Ovče Pole. Assuming that the Ottoman units north of Kumanovo were merely forward detachments, it was ordered to the Ottoman troops to continue their advance towards south, as previously planned. After midnight, it received a report from Danube Division I which stated that the division was attacked by the strong enemy forces and suffered heavy casualties, but at that moment it was too late for any change of orders. On the other side, Zeki Pasha decided to continue the attack with the hope that his forces would be able to achieve victory on the following day. The Ottoman attack on their right wing started around 5:30. VI Corps was assigned to tie up as many enemy forces as possible by attacking from the front, while Štip Infantry Division was again assigned to flank attack. Danube Division I again had to withstand heavy pressure, but around 10:00 parts of Danube Division II arrived from the rear and strengthened the defense. At the same time, Cavalry Division moved to the left bank of Pčinja and slowed the advance of Ottoman forces towards Srtevica. Around 12:00, parts of Danube Division II reinforced the defense of Srtevica, definitely stopping the advance of the Ottoman right wing.

On the left Ottoman wing, a lot of reservists from Üsküb Infantry Division had deserted during the night, upon hearing that the Third Army had captured Pristina and that it is marching towards Skopje. Still, at 5:30, VII Corps started the attack. However, Morava Division I counterattacked at 6:00 and with the arrival of Timok Division II from the rear they forced the entire Ottoman left wing to retreat. Around 9:30, Drina Division II from the rear echelon of the First Army arrived to the front and attacked the Ottoman center. Around 11:00, Monastir Infantry Division started to retreat. The commander of VI Corps managed to temporarily halt the Serbian advance by using his last reserves, but in the repeated attack around 13:00, Drina Division I captured Zebrnjak hill, the main object in Ottoman defense and forced 17th Infantry Division to retreat. With Üsküb /Skopje/ Infantry Division and Monastir Infantry Division already retreating, the battle was resolved. At 15:00, Morava Division I entered Kumanovo. Ottoman forces retreated in disorder: VII and parts of VI Corps towards Skopje and V and parts of VI Corps towards Stip and Veles. Serbian troops missed the chance to pursue them.

The Ottoman Vardar Army fought the Kumanovo battle according to plan, but despite it suffered a heavy defeat. Although Zeki Pasha operationally surprised the Serbian command by his sudden attack, the decision to act offensively against the superior enemy was a grave error which determined the outcome of Battle of Kumanovo. On the other side, the Serbian command started the battle without plans and preparations, and missed the chance to pursue the defeated enemy and effectively end the operations in Vardar Macedonia, although it had the fresh troops of the rear echelon available for such action. Even after the end of the Kumanovo battle, the Serbs still believed that it was fought against weaker Ottoman units and that main enemy forces were on Ovce Pole.

Nevertheless, the Battle of Kumanovo was a decisive factor in the outcome of the war in Macedonia.

The Ottoman plan for an offensive war had failed, and the Vardar Army was forced to abandon much territory and lost a significant number of artillery pieces without the possibility to reinforce, because the supply routes from Anatolia were cut. The Vardar Army was not able to organize the defense on Vardar River and was forced to abandon Skopje, retreating all the way to Prilep. The First Army advanced slowly and entered Skopje on 26 October. Two days later, it was strengthened by Morava Division II, while the rest of the Third Army was sent to Metohija and then through northern Albania to the Adriatic coast. The Second Army was sent to aid the Bulgarians in the Siege of Adrianople Edirne, while the First Army was preparing for an offense towards Prilep and Bitola.

The end of the long-lasting Turkish administration in the Balkans is connected with the Serb victory during the Kumanovo Battle near Kumanovo in 1912 in the First Balkan War, and the merits for the brilliantly achieved outcome should be granted to Ahmed Ademovic, the Roma soldier and trumpeter from Leskovac. In the moment when the outcome of the Kumanovo Battle was uncertain, Ahmed secretly approached the back of the Turkish Army and played on his trumpet tones for retreat according to his skills and knowledge. The confused Turkish Army which was at that moment in fierce rush, and started to retreat. Then Ahmed also secretly left the position of the Turkish army and played on his trumpet a signal for the Serb attack. His gesture was one of the crucial factors for the Serb victory in this battle. This behavior of Ahmed was studied in the military academies. The victory of Serbian Army was mortifying discomfiture for the Turks which provided space for the future Serb advancing along the Vardar River valley. Particularly for this action, Ahmed received a honorable Order of Karađorđe's Star which is the highest civilian and military decoration of Serbia. And his simple deed ended and remains in books on the French and Russian military academies as the positive example of trickery of an ordinary soldier.

Kumanovo Battle was an important Serbian victory over the Ottoman Army in Vardar Macedonia, shortly after the outbreak of the First Balkan war which marked the beginning of the liberation of South East Europe from the Ottoman Empire. The *Balkan alliance* preceded the liberation war against the Ottoman Empire, as well as the correlated agreements between the Balkans countries Serbia, Montenegro, Bulgaria and Greece. The First Balkan war made end to the long lasting process in Europe suppression of the Osman Empire from Europe, which started by the defeat of Kara Mustafa in Vienna in 1683. Kumanovo Battle was the significant historical moment for Serbia and the Serbian people in general, probably for Europe also, as its outcome was liberation of the *Stara Srbija Old Serbia areas, which comprise the Stara Raška, Kosovo and Metohija and Skopje-Tetovo domains*. After the defeat in the Kumanovo Battle, the Ottoman army abandoned the major part of Vardar Macedonia, suffering heavy losses in manpower and in war material. During the Kumanovo battle two days of fierce combat, with extensive bloody affairs in Nagoricane villages and around the Zebrnjak hill, the First army experienced 687 casualties, 3208 wounded and 597 missing officers and soldiers. The entire troop of the Dunav Division its soldiers of the 1st Troop of the 2nd Battalion all got killed in the campaigns during the Kumanovo Battle on the Zebrnjak site, on 23rd October 1912. This troop was mostly formed by population of the Drmno village near Kostolac who all gave their lives for the Fatherland in the Kumanovo Battle. It was estimated that the Turkish loss in Kumanovo Battle counted 12000 soldiers, of which 2000 men were imprisoned.

Present day only ruined lower part of the Zebrnjak memorial monument remained, housing in the charnel-house /ossuary/ the bones of the 687 Serbian soldiers killed in the Kumanovo battle, which were kept in the nearby Saint George Monastery until brought here. The three sided pyramid tower of the original Zebrnjak Monument is missing which made its height of 48.5 meters. The original Zebrnjak Monument was destroyed in May 1942 by the Bulgarian army during the Second World War. By its monumental architecture and appearance, Zebrnjak Monument was one of a kind in the Balkans. Zebrnjak Monument was constructed from basalt rocks/granite cubes, according to the project designed by *Momir P. Korunovich* and the frescoes in the interior were painted by *Zivorad Nastasijevich*, on them were represented pictures from everyday life with figures wearing Serbian folklore clothing. In regard with its unique appearance, the Zebrnjak monument in Kumanovo striven to achieve the traditional style of architecture, by decorative elements of the Serbian Medieval sacral architecture. Restoration of the Zebrnjak Monument glorifying and commemorating the Kumanovo Battle is celebration of the Serbian Army victory, which does not belong only to Serbs, but to all the Balkan allies, and makes the clear sign that Belgrade and Skopje had opened new door toward the future, founding primarily on the honest faith into freedom and the common power of the mutual trust.

Lesnovo Monastery

Lesnovo Monastery was built in the tiny village of Lesnovo, close to Kratovo and Zletovo settlements in north-eastern Macedonia. The Lesnovo Monastery is likewise many other Serbian medieval monasteries in present North Macedonia located secluded up a long and imposing mountain road at the elevation of nearly 1000 meters, on the south-western slopes of the Osogovo Mountains. The Church in Lesnovo is dedicated to the Archistrategos Michael and the Holy Archangel Gabriel and has been built built between 1341 and 1349. The Lesnovo Monastery is the largest and best preserved among the Serbian Medieval endowments of the 14th century in the Balkans and one the *most visually stunning and culturally significant monasteries of present North Macedonia*. The historical importance of the Lesnovo Monastery is above all as a *monastic-spiritual, literary and copying center*, of equal importance.

The Church of the Lesnovo Monastery was built on the foundations of an earlier/older shrine that existed in the 11th century during the time of the *Vulnerable hermit Gabriel of Lesnovo whose ascetic cave cell is set nearby*. The Church of Lesnovo is dedicated to *Saint Archangel Gabriel and hermit Gabriel of Lesnovo*. The older-original monastery dating from the 11th century was extended and thoroughly rebuilt in 1331 by Despot-duke Jovan Oliver, the prominent representative of the Serbian aristocracy and the master of Ovce Pole and Lesnovo region on which testify the carved inscriptions above the former entrance door. The Duke Jovan Oliver was a military leader of Emperor Dusan of Serbia and one of the most powerful Serbian lords of the second half of the 14th century, and the owner of large estates in what is today eastern North Macedonia. Duke Jovan Oliver was one among many Serbian noblemen who ruled the territory of present North Macedonia in the Middle Ages and sponsored construction of a number of valuable churches.

At the Church Assembly in Skopje in 1347 Tzar Dusan proclaimed Lesnovo Monastery for the seat of the newly established Bishopric of Zletovo. In 1381 the Lesnovo Monastery was granted to Hilandar-Chilandary Monastery as its *metochion /church property/*. Lesnovo Monastery boasts the rich Treasury with numerous precious sacral manuscripts and liturgical and religious books. The conception of space, similar to that which was characteristic of architecture in Greece, remained constant in the works of Lesnovo Monastery masters. The concept "similar" could also be used for the overall structures of the edifices, and particularly for their exteriors, which leads one to the conclusion that the planning was in the hands of informed patrons who were in contact with each other. It is also possible to assume that a single group of craftsmen was at work here, traveling from one site to the next. Their knowledge and practice originated from somewhere between those trends found in the Byzantine capital /or in Thessaloniki using the concepts existing in Constantinople/ and the architecture style found in the western territories of Greece, primarily in Epirus. Therein, the long tradition of Serbian architecture in the conception of the entire structure of Lesnovo Monastery was respected: the grouping of areas into a closed entirety, and attention to proportions with an emphasis on the vertical aspects of the structure.

The church of the *Holy Archangel Gabriel in Lesnovo* /built in 1341, narthex added by Duke Jovan Oliver in 1349 who restored and expanded the older the 11th century monastery/ has parts of two different architectural conceptions: a church in the narrow sense and the inner and outer narthexes. The Lesnovo church is done as an enclosed whole, marked by rhythmical series of decorative arches which are two staged and placed in two zones, one above the other. The concept of the semi-circular pillars which are joined to the pilasters, hinted at in the church of the Archangels Monastery in Stip is materialized consistently at Lesnovo Monastery. It originates either directly or by way of Thessaloniki-Salonica, from the Byzantine capital. Without fail, the concept of the narthex of the Lesnovo Monastery can be attributed to a representative source. With its masterfully built structure, featuring the cupola in the center, wide open walls, the bi-fora and other details in the facade-work, Lesnovo Monastery is very close to those works coming from the best of Byzantine workshops. As a whole, Lesnovo Monastery was a model for *Psaca Monastery* /1358, founded by Sevastokrator lord Vlatko Paskac/.

Along with details that indicate the best of construction workshops, such as the shape of the apse and the semi- circular niches on its external walls, the work on the decorative surfaces is also remarkable, accompanied by colorful traits characteristic of the architecture of the late Byzantine world. The death scene of Saint Gabriel of Lesnovo was painted in a specially constructed shallow niche in the lateral altar wall of the church in the Monastery Lesnovo. The tendency toward decoration, color and ornamentation, construction with the support of brick and mortar, is shown to the greatest extent on the facade surfaces of Zaum Monastery /on Lake Ohrid, 1361, founded by lord Kesar Grguric/. The complex of Lesnovo Monastery was built in the traditional Serbian-Byzantine school. Thus, the Lesnovo church reflects the ideas that came about in the Paleologus Renaissance, and hints the innovations which would be created in the forthcoming periods of Serbian architecture. In 1342 the Lesnovo Monastery was connected directly with Mount Athos which was the time when lord Jovan Oliver has given the monastery under jurisdiction of Hilandar-Chillandary monastery

The fresco-decoration of Lesnovo Monastery is work of four authors. In regard with wonderfully preserved details and variety of scenes, the Lesnovo Monastery frescoes comprise the horizon of the Byzantine painting and rank among the *most magnificent artistic achievements at the beginning of the 14th century*. The whole interior of the Lesnovo temple is full with frescoes which were painted in two stages: first in the time between 1341 and 1346, and the second in 1347/48 and 1349. Among the Lesnovo Monastery fresco ensemble, the painted portraits of the *founder Despot Jovan Oliver and his wife Marija*, the portraits of the *Serbian Tsar Stefan Dušan and Queen Elena, fresco of Archangel Michael on a horse and of the monk Gavriil* /also and the hermits saints of Joakim Osogovski and Prohor Pčinski/ are outstanding. Portrait of

Tsar Dušan dominates by its size as it is larger than the Christ itself and the saints surrounding him. On the ceiling of the inner narthex you can see frescoes of the sun and the moon and 12 animals of people in the sky. Despite they clearly show the zodiac signs, it is believed that they are not designed to depict the zodiac signs. The icon-painters of Lesnovo Monastery have left their signature on small circle fields. The inscription on the fresco of the Lesnovo Monastery on which the landowner Jovan Oliver is depicted provides significant data on appellation this person was attributed in different periods. The precise, clear drawing with reach ornamentation and color is expressed on the frescoes with the figure of Archangel Michael, on the portrait of the donor of the church and the scenes with the "Scab patients", "Dormition of Virgin", "Michail saves Constantinople from Saracens" and others. The khetotorial arrangements are depicted in the foundation commissioned by the members on the nobility.

From the Lesnovo Monastery fresco-decorations of the inner narthex the ones that stand out are the compositions from the life of Christ and the acts of Saints, as well as the illustrations of David's psalms. The portraits of Tzar Dusan and Empress Elena are among the most monumental in the medieval fresco-painting. For the first time in this presentation the Son of God appears, unlike the usual one where the angels are the ones playing the role of distributing wreaths. Inside the Lesnovo Monastery, the fresco of a paralytic boy guiding the blind man painted in 1347, immediately draws one's attention: the spotted skin of the leprous man and the boy is in stark contrast to the divine depictions of saints and angels on the walls. On one of the fresco of the Lesnovo Monastery there is the Serbian Kolo dance painted, with dances whose hands are interwoven. Artistically, the figures of Lesnovo Monastery are modeled with tranquil grace and strong facial features. The flowing and airy fabrics of the figures superimposed on the visual perspective of the background add depth to the whole scene.

One of the highlights of the Lesnovo Monastery is highly rich and beautifully wood carved iconostasis from the 19th century, carved in walnut by *Miyak masters led by Petre Filipovski – Garkata*. The Lesnovo iconostasis is the oldest of the three preserved iconostasis completed by these masters woodcarvers the icosnostasis of the Sveti Jovan Bigorski Monastery and the Skopje Church of the Holy Savior Sveti Spas Church in Skopje.

Mariovo Morihovo

Mariovo /also Morihovo/ is the mountainous region in southern Macedonia, actually the southernmost part of Macedonia, at the foot of the Kajmakcalan peak, known for its natural beauties and rich cultural legacy famous for uniquely wonderful white traditional costumes. The Mariovo area in present North Macedonia is somewhat large but since there has been no urban development in these spaces over the past century, this region contains no actual urban settlements and towns, but only rustic villages that represent one of the most distinctive ethnic clarity and common identity of the Orthodox Slavic population in Macedonia. Mariovo is situated at the average elevation of 1050 meters, between the mountains Selechka (highest peak Visoka 1471 m) on the west, Nidze Mt (highest peak Kajmakchalan 2520 m) and Kozhuf (highest peak Zelenbeg 2171 m) on the south, Kozjak (highest peak Baltova Chuka 1822 m) in the east and Dren (mountain) (highest peak Studenica 1663 m) in the north. Those majestic mountains of Mariovo area divide the *Vardar part of Macedonia from the Aegean part of Macedonia*. The largest village in Mariovo is *Vitolište*, situated in Prilep's municipality. Mariovo is nowadays divided in three municipalities. Konopishte is in Kavadarci municipality, Vitolishte in

Prilep municipality, and Staravina in Novaci municipality, as a part of Bitola's county.

Nidže Mt is mountain in south Macedonia, along which goes the border with Greece. The highest peak of the Nidze Mountain is Kajmakčalan, 2521 meters. Mountain Nidže had been created by fissure in Tertiary and comes in Paleosoic slate, while in its highest part it features some Mesosoic characteristics. Mountain Nidže is known by richness of forests, mountain pastures and diversified flora. Nidže Mountain spreads on the border between Macedonia and Greece, east of Pelagonija valley, and on the eastern slope it is almost precipitous. Towards northwest the Nidže Mountain borders the Skočivir Ravine, while the Crna reka /Black River/ joins in large bend with the Satoka River, which further flows in direction of more than 90 degrees southeast to its junction with the Gradashtanska River.

Despite centuries of dispute over who owns Macedonia, a part of this recently independent state remains of great historical significance to Serbs. During World War I, from 12th September until the 3rd October 1916, the Battle of Kajmakcalan between the Serbian and Bulgarian-German troops took place at Kajmakčalan peak and around the adjacent peaks, resulting in the great Serbian victory. The Nidže mountain changed hands several times, but eventually the Bulgarian and German foes were driven back, and the Eastern Front saw a change in the course of the Great War. Yet nothing could prepare visitors for its breathtaking beauty, quietness and solitude, in contrast to the intolerable noise of the battle that raged there nearly 100 years ago. Valiant and heroic Serbian combat ended the bloodiest battle of the whole Salonica campaign with liberation of Bitola /Monastir/ within the Salonika front, and had marked the beginning of the successful outcome of the First World War. The Serbs won, but they payed a very high price around 10.000 Serbian casualties and wounded. There is a tiny church dedicated to Saint Elias Sveti Ilija made up of weapons, shells and barbed wire fence off the church, in a testament to eternal peace and a crypt for the Serbian soldiers who heroically died in the battle. In the church there is an urn which contains the *heart of Dr. Archibald Reiss*, the Swiss-German father of Forensic Medicine, who sought to bring to the world's attention the *slaughter of Serbian civilians during the Great War*. It says :

"In this urn, On Kajmakčalan's peak, The golden heart sleeps, Of a Serbian friend, 8th August 1929".

Such was Reiss's loyalty to the Serbian cause that he fought alongside Serbs, lived in Belgrade until his death, and declared in his will that his heart be embalmed and placed in an urn on Kajmakčalan. This testament to the indescribably heroic Serbian history is not that well known, and deserves not to remain a secret, but to gain constant admiration of the world as the legacy of Serbs among the mountains of Macedonia.

All around the mountains of Mariovo and on the Nidze Mountain are settled semi-slavicized Wallachians cattle-breeders, and in the nearby Meglen are are continuously settled the *Meglen Wallachians*. Wallachians of the Meglen area are recorded in a document of the Holy Atos Monastery archive in 1094, while Tache Papagahi, Originea Munovistenilor si Gopesenilor, Bucuresti, 1935 analyses characteristics of the local Tsintsar /Aromanian/ dialect, and consider the Gopes and Maloviste villages as the original pra-habitation and homeland of the Meglen-Wallachian lanugauge of the original population. The Meglen Wallachian live in the prefectures of Pella and Kukes of the present Greece, in the village of Hum, Konsko and Sermenin in present Macedonia. Unlike their Wallachian brothers Aromunians Tsintsars, Karakachans and Farsheriotes, the Meglen Wallachians were never nomad cattle-breeders, but the peasants engaged in agriculture.

The Mariovo region was settled by the Serbs persecuted from Greece and Albania after the Balkan wars and the First World War large number of Serbs settlers, especially from the mountainous areas and the valleys from Prespa and Ohrid, as well as refugees from the Serbian lands in Korca and Elbasan and Ianina in Epir /data from 1927/.

It is said that Mariovo was named after the beautiful and brave girl Marija. The legend says that some Turkish Pasha who has conquered the villages of Mariovo, has fallen in love with this girl and, enchanted by her beauty, was prepared to do everything to gain her love. But Marija's father was not approving on it, because his daughter was a Christian, and the Turk was a Muslim. The Pasha would not give up. Marija had answered his persistence with one condition: she would become his wife, but the entire region, from the Poloski monastery, Selecka mountain, to the village by the name of Brod, then the Bitola region, the Nidze mountain and to the reach of Kozjak, to remain Christian and that not a single Turk should be inhabited there. The Pasha agreed to this condition, signed papers on that decision and took Marija with him. He took her on the rood leading to the village of Dunje, Marija suddenly took the knife from her folds, and forcefully killed herself. Taking away her life, she did not surrender to the pasha, who later, although he wanted to, could not annul the contract he previously signed. By the power of this document, the guarantee that the entire region should remain Christian was respected. In the honor of the girl and her courageous act, and the love for her fellow people, the region was named Mariovo.

The church of "Saint Nicholas" in the village of Monastery in Mariovo is built on an older facility, and it got today shape in 1266. The church is a three nave basilica without narthex, central vessel is arched and the sides are with an open roof construction. The east parts end with semi-circular apse from the inside and three side apse from the outside. Fresco painting of Saint Nicholas Monastery in Mariovo was completed in 1271 during the reign of Michael VIII Palaeologus. The long article in the main part explains the history of the church. It says that the painting was done under the leadership of Deacon John, the Holy Archbishop speaker, who called several prominent masters to do the frescoes of the church.

Marko's Monastery Susica

The Marko's Monastery with the church dedicated to Saint Demetrius is situated at the edge of the Sušica village, on the left bank of the Markova Reka River /Marko's River/, on the Kitka Mountains, some 20 kilometers south of Skopje. Marko's Monastery ofSaint Demetrius was founded in 1345 by the *Serbian King Vukashin Mrnjavcevic* and completed in 1366 by his son *King Marko* who donated the frescoes painted between 1366 and 1371 and after whose cult the Monastery got its name. On this testify depictions of kings Vukasin and Marko painted in the outer porch by the southern entrance to the church.

The architecture of the Saint Demetrius church of the Marko's Monastery has been built of layers of bricks and stone, in the basis of single inscribed cross with a central dome and a blind dome in the narthex. It has the original iconstasis completed of stone pillars. Interior of the Saint Demetrios church of the Marko Monastery is decorated with eight-sided stone columns. The elegant exo-narthex (open porch) of the Marko's Monastery was added in 1830 by *Hamzi Pasha*, who as the Turkish aristocrat generously donated the Christian monastery throughout the 19th century, which was quite surprising. Marko's Monastery is the burial church of the Mrnjavcevic Family and belongs to the most important Medieval spiritual centers of original Stara Serbia Old Serbia in the present North Macedonia.

The well preserved frescoes of the Saint Demetrius Marko's Monastery have been painted by several artists of different skills, probably by painters from Ohrid, under patterns of the Thessaloniki and Constantinople master painters. The fresco-painting in the church of Saint Demetrius belongs to the Byzantine painting patterns achieved in Old Serbia-Macedonia the second half of the 14th century. The tendency for adding dramatization and narrative painting of the scenes is visible. The content of the Marko's Monastery fresco-painting consists of numerous cycles: The Cherubim hymns on the Divine Service, The Akathistos of the Holy Virgin, Miracles and Parables, hagiographies of St. Nicholas and St. Demetrius, The Rachel Weeping of slaying the Bethlehem children, Divine Liturgy in the Altar, Angels and Demons on the columns. The painter's skillfulness was expressed by the Holy warrior St Demetrius wearing magnificent cloths and riding a horse depicted above the entrance of the church. St Demetrius known as guard, defender of God from various enemies and natural disasters is blessed by Christ Emanuel and angels are landing carrying his helmet, sword, shield and arrow, the armor and armored gloves and the martyr wreath. The scenes depicted in the dome of narthex Heaven with Christ Pantocrator, Table with Christ Logos and The Ascension of the Virgin Mary reveal the hidden meanings in the complex ideology in the medieval Christian art. The portraits of kings Volkashin and Marko wearing royal cloths and holding unfolded scrolls with written texts in which they are stated as donors are depicted in the life size on the southern facade of the Marko's Monastery and make best preserved depictions of the Mrnjavchevic family rulers.

The inscription above the southern entrance, inside the Saint Demetrius church of the Marko's Monastery, written in Church-Slavic language is considered one of the most important documents, containing data about the construction of the church and its donors *Faithful king Volkasin and the queen Elena and their very much beloved daughters and sons, the faithful princes Marko and Andreaš, Ivaniš and Dimitar*. This inscription was written after King Vukašin died in the Battle on Maritza River in 1371, when Marko as the first born son became king.

During the Ottoman era, in 1467/8 the Marko's Monastery has been recorded as having 20 monks. The Marko's Monastery prior Kiril Pejčinovik put a great deal of effort for its development as a spiritual center. By its hand-copying role during the Medieval era, Marko's Monastery is considered as one of the most significant spiritual centers of Orthodoxy. After Abbott Kiril left in 1818, the monastic life was interrupted, the monastery properties were forcefully taken and destroyed, and the fresco-paintings were white-washed and repainted. Marko's Monastery is nowadays given its previous, representative appearance after the thorough conservation and restoration works fresco-paintings and the church architecture are restored, and monastery dormitories and the dining room were reconstructed, making it one of the most valuable cultural heritage of Macedonia.

It needs an half hour walk from Susica village to get to the Marko's Monastery.

Matejce Monastery

The Matejce Monastery or the *Mateic Monastery* is the Serbian Medieval Monastery situated in the historical Zegligovo area, at the foot of the Skopska Crna Gora mountains, close to the town of Kumanovo, some 20 km from the center of Skopje, at the outskirts of the village of *South or Old Serbia* bearing the same name the Matejce village. The history of this monastery is very interesting, which in the past was also called the Zegligovo Monastery. It was erected already in the 11th century, with the interesting feature of the monastic church dedicated to the Birth of the Holy Virgin bearing some preserved inscriptions in Greek language which date from the time of the Byzantine tsar Isaac I Komnenos (1057-1059). However, in the historical archives this monastery is first mentioned in the founding charter of the Serbian king Milutin (1282-1321) from 1300 who was its khtetor-donor. The Tsar Dusan carried out thorough reconstruction of original foundations of the Matejce Monastery, which was completed after his death in 1355 by his wife Empress Jelena and thier son Uros. The Church of the Matejce Monastery is dedicated to the Ascension of the Holy Virgin. Back in his day, this monastery becomes a kind of center of spirituality and events in the Serbian medieval state. According to the sources we see that Emperor Dusan and Tsarina Jelena often stayed here and that various Serbian convocations and congregations were held. Emperor Dušan's son, Serbian Emperor Uros (1355-1371) and his wife Ana completed a thorough reconstruction of the Matejce Monastery around 1357, after which it became the endowment of Emperor Uros. That's when the Matejce Monastery got its present shape and appearance.

"In the 14th century, the Serbian kings and the Serbian high dignitaries and nobility had erected numerous churches that made the Serbian arts here achieved the pinnacle. Around Skopje, Prizren, Prilep, Kuystendil nowadays in western Bulgaria, Kumanovo, Kratovo, Štip, Strumica, in the Valley of Crna Reka, the masses of the Serbian churches appeared. In the areas of Tetovo, Debar, Ohrid, Korca, Prespa, Bitolj, Florina, Ostrova, Kostur, Serez and Drama, there were numerous Serbian churches founded..."
Catena mundi Predrag R. Dragic Kijuk

The last significant religious structure built during the reign of the Tsar Dusan, the Matejce church dedicated to the Ascension of the Holy Virgin, was completed after the tsar's death /1355/. The Matejce church remained severely ruined during its long history, on the dominated peak of the Skopska Crna Gora, in the vicinity of Kumanovo. This Medieval structure of significant dimensions features basis of elongated inscribed cross and the facade built of ashlar stones, with five domes and a small inner narthex. In its basis and the upper construction the Matejce church represents the classical sample of the Byzantine architectural principle of the 11th and the 12th century. The spacious and well-lighted church of the Matejce Monastery, with a dome of larger diameter than in Visoki Decani Monastery, stands for the Constantinople manners of harmonized well-lit space which complies to the harmony of calm and static masses. On the eastern part of the Matejce church there are three semicircular apses. Contrary to the other Serbian churches of this area of Macedonia the South Serbia of this historical period, the church of the Matejce Monastery has a particular feature the tympanum of the central dome has 12 sides and 12 windows.

Traditional architecture of the Matejce Monastery church does not reflect the other examples of the churches built during the reign of Tsar Dusan. It is surely the work of Greek masters who do not build elongated basis, nor use the vertical of the upper construction, that are common in the Serbian architecture of the 14th century. The political particularity that flamed during the reign of incapable son of Tsar Dusan tsar Uros /1355-1371/ had greatly left traces in the religious architecture of Serbia. Not any significant ruler's endowment was built in those years, and some later data testify that Tsar Uros rebuilt the main church of Skopje /without any traces left nowadays/, and he might be the only ruler of the Nemanide Dynasty who did not erect a single church.

The Matejce Monastery is the last large Serbian Medieval church with preserved frescoes that testify on the hardship of historical events after the death of Tsar Dusan, with fresco decoration completed around 1355/1356. The pretty destroyed frescoes of the

Matejce Monastery represent the end of the encyclopedic tendencies of the Serbian paintings of the 14th century. The frescoes of the Matejce Monastery are very comprehensive, but not particularly complex. Frescoes of the Holy Virgin church of the Matejce Monastery feature a number of cycles : the Great Feasts, Parables and the Earthen life of the Christ, Christ Passions, Life of the Holy Virgin, Acts of the Apostles, Miracles of the Apostles, Legends of the Holy hermits Antonius and Makarios, Legends of the Saint Demetrius of Thessaloniki, Scenes of Life of Saint Elias, Cycles of the Ecumenical councils with addition of the Serbian council of King Stefan, the Christmas Epistle of Saint John Damascin, the Lineage of Jesse, the Lineage of the ruling dynasties of Comnenos Asen and Nemanides-Nemanjic. Besides the mentioned scenes, in the altar apse of the Matejce Monastery are painted common liturgical themes, and numerous single depictions, and portraits of the Empress Jelena and Tsar Uros holding the model of the church and handling it to the Holy Virgin, and depiction of an Abbott of the Matejce Monastery.

After the Turkish conquest the Matejce Monastery was destroyed and declined, and in the 18th century the lead roof was moved and used for construction of the Eski Mosque in Kumanovo. After the Balkan wars the Monastery of Matejce became part of the Kingdom of Serbia. The Matejce Monastery was rebuilt between two world wars, but its original church was unfortunately demolished. After the Second WW the new restoration was carried out in the Matejce Monastery, in 1960.

The Serbian Orthodox Church officially has jurisdiction over the Orthodox community in Macedonia. The self-proclaimed independent Macedonian Orthodox Church had appeared in 1964 when the Macedonian dioceses split from its jurisdictional unity with the Serbian Orthodox Church. Although the great number /or majority/ of the Medieval Orthodox churches in Macedonia had been built by the Serbian Medieval kings and nobility in the Middle ages, the fact is that the modern Macedonian historians systematically misinterpret and avoid, but let this heritage be endangered and experience considerable destruction, and a target of numerous attacks, both in the past and in recent times..... The Matejce Monastery was destroyed in 2001 by Albanian terrorists who used the church during their rebellion as the headquarter, ammunition storage and the training center. This resulted in severe damage of Matejce Monastery frescoes and parts of the church, particularly the altar space, when the dormitory /that was previously used for children camps/ was thorn down. At present, the village of Matejce where the Matejce Monastery is located is populated by majority of Albanian inhabitants (85%), with only some 350 Serbs (10%).

Matka Canyon

Matka is the narrow canyon of the lower course of the Treska River, located 15 km southwest of Skopje, covering roughly 5,000 hectares of the beautiful artificial Matka lake with the Hydro-power Plant Sveti Andreja, steep sides of mountains that are 1000 meters high and challenging caves and picturesque Medieval Monasteries. The famous architect dr Miladin Pecinar, was the designer of the project of construction of Hydro-power Plant of Sveti Andreja, as was the first name of this important energetic facility near Skopje, who was also the head of monitoring body of the complete building process. Construction works started in 1935 and the Hydro-power Plant of Matka started its operations in 1938. This unique energetic facility of Yugoslavia was part of the development campaign of the capital of Republic of Macedonia. The main architect Miladin Pecinar firmly noticed all beauties of the Treska River Canyon, and put much efforts and did his best and succeeded in preservation of its most important features. The Arh Dam of the Matka Hydro-power Plant is unique in the world, with in-built belts, completely independent one from the other. In such construction, if one of the belt fails, there is not any possibility of a general hazard. The full capacity of the Matka Hydro-power plant was five times larger than the needs for energy in Skopje of that time, as this hydro-power plant greatly provided development and growth of the city of Skopje in the 20th century. The Matka Hydro-power plant was one of the stragegic targets during the Second WW, where fierce battles were waged. The Matka Hydro-power Plant was bombed in war attacks, during withdrawal of Fascists. The Matka HE several times saved the city of Skopje from floods, especialy during the huge floodings in 1962 and in 1979 when the dam prevented a large flood inflow and terrible consequences and a catastrophy was avoided.

Matka Canyon is home to a wide variety of plants and animals, some of which is unique to the area. The Matka Canyon is home to 77 endemic species of butterfly. The caves of Matka Canyon are home to large populations of bats. Taking a boat ride along the Matka Canyon you can enjoy magnificent surroundings, the scents of flora and the songs of the numerous birds that live there. If you are lucky you will be able to see some wild animals like ducklings swimming in the Lake or a wild boar, a hare or similar animals.

Matka Canyon is among the most popular outdoor destinations in Macedonia and one of Macedonia's foremost areas for alpine hiking. The climbing season in Matka Canyon begins around Easter and finishes in November. Kayaking on the Treska River which forms a wonderful lake is a popular activity, as are fishing, hunting and swimming. There are 10 caves within the Matka Canyon, with the shortest that is 20 meters long and the longest one, Vrelo Cave being 193 meters long, considered the longest cave in Macedonia. The Matka Canyon also features two vertical pits, both roughly extending 35 meters in depth. Matka Canyon is home to several picturesque Medieval monasteries /*St Nicholas Monastery, St*

Andrew's Monastery, Matka Monastery The Holy Virgin Monastery, Sveta Nedela, Sveti Spas, Sveti Jovan Zlatousti and others/. In the very Matka Canyon, just beside the Saint Andrew Monastery there is the popular restaurant with 80 seats inside and 400 seats in the beautiful garden, serving delicious authentic Macedonian food. It comprises the nice traditionally furnished hotel with 5 comfortable and clean rooms, all with private facilities, categorized with high A category. The rooms are equipped with shower cabins, toilette, LCD TV, satellite channels, fast free wireless Internet 24/7. The Matka hotel has a king's apartment with open-air Jacuzzi, toilet, LCD TV with satellite channels, fast wireless Internet 24/7 (without additional fee), mini bar and all the conveniences which one apartment of such kind offers.

The *Monastery of St. Nicholas Shishovski* is interesting monastic site situated on top of a high cliff above the Lake of Matka on the left side, giving the visitor a spectacular and memorable view of the Saint Andrew Monastery, the lake and its surroundings of the Treska River. The terrain around the Shishovski Monastery is completely inaccessivle for cars, and it can be reached only on foot by 3 paths from the bridge over the Treska River and the village of Matka /some half an hour of walk/, of from the Sisevo village /1 hour of walk/, or from the top of the Vodno Mountain /walk of some 2,5 hours/. It is 18 km away from the city of Skopje, and some 3 km from the Sisevo village. Just across the lake and the Shishovski Monastery the magic view spreads to the Saint Andrew which is believed to have been erected by the legendary Prince Marko.

There is no precise information when the St Nicholas Shishovski Monastery was built, however it is known that it was first mentioned in the 17th century. Unfortunately, during the 18th century the monastery was abandoned, only to be resettled the following century. Close to both monasteries of St. Andrew's and of St. Nicholas there is the Matka Monastery dating from the 14th century, its frescoes dating from the 15th century. Frescoes that remained express sublimation of the human ugliness in subtle and formally artistic effectiveness. Very experienced in drawing and painting monks-painters depict heads of saints almost as caricatures, with large noses, sunk cheeks and small suspicious eyes but in rich colors and in strong expressions of dark shades and nervous reflections of light. Between two world wars, there in the village of Sisevo lived an old and reputed mohammedan Memedovic Family. Suleyman Memedovic was in 1926 elected for the mayor of the Sisevo Municipality. In his youth his father married the Orthodox Christian wife, who made their son Suleyman fond of the Christian ancestors and the Shisevo Monastery. This was the reason that Suleyman became the Serb komita who took part in numerous fierce battles against the Bulgarians and the Turks. Although of islamic faith, such a pious man donated reconstruction of the St Nicholas Sisovski Monastery. Besides the reconstructed church, he built large dormitories and hospices for monks and visitors.

Saint Andrew's Monastery is beautifully fresco painted Serbian Medieval church situated in the wonderful gorge of the Treska River, on Matka Lake, 17 km away from Skopje. Saint Andrew's Monastery was built in 1389 by the youngest son of the Serbian King Vukasin Mrnjavcevic, *King Andrija Andrew*, who ruled the area around Prilep in the 14th century. Monastery of Saint Andrew was painted with frescoes of high artistic quality by the Metropolitan Jovan and monk Gregory, who accomplished the special quality of the experienced and technically outstanding iconography in three zones of the church. Mitropolitan Jovan also painted frescoes of Zrze Monastery in Prilep, and probably was educated in Constantinople. The Standing SS Archangel and Gabriel are painted in the first zone. Apostles and Evangelists Mark, Matthew, John and Lucas are depicted in the southern conch. On the southern wall are painted the Holy Warriors George and Demtrius. On the western wall, south from the entrance to the Saint Andrew Monastery Church is Archangel Michael depicted, while Archangel Gabriel is painted north from the entrance. The Holy Warriors Theodor Stratilat and Theodor Tyron are presented on the northern wall. In the southern conch are Apostles Paul, Andrew, Peter and the Holy Mother Zastapnica depicted. Between the first and the second zone of Saint Andrew Monastery frescoes are painted busts of monks and saints. In the second zone of frescoes of Saint Andrew Monastery are depictions of Christ Passions, that begin with the Secret Dinner in the apse. On the western wall is Assumption of the Holy Mother of God painted. In the third zone of frescoes are the Major Feasts which start with the Birth of the Christ, painted in the apse. In the northern conch of the apse are scenes of the Crucifixion and the Descent to Hell. On the pandantives are depicted Evangelists and in the tambour Prophets. The Holy Virgin with Christ child and the Holy Liturgy of Arch Hierarchs is painted the altar space. The impressive figures of the four Holy Warriors guard the entrance to the St Andrew church.

Frescoes of Saint Andrew Monastery distinguish themselves by their style, but their iconography also differentiate from the other Medieval monuments of Macedonia. Frescoes in the narthex added later after the church construction, were painted in 1559-60. Painters of the St Andrew Church succeeded in leaving the Byzantine iconography and depicted figures of the Holy Warriors in their full sizes, instead of depictions of the Holy Hermits and Jesus miracles and scenes from life of the Holy Virgin, which was a significant step in resolving the perspective and location of figures and portraits within the limited space.

Matka Monastery, or Monastery of the Holy Mother of God, built in the 14th century, is located on the left bank of the Treska River. According to an inscription above the church entrance, someone named Milica found the church, which was in poor condition and without a roof in 1497. She replaced the roof, added new frescoes, built a portico and created vineyards of the Monastery. Some reparation works were carried out at the end of the 19th century. The church of Matka Monastery has the form of a narrow inscribed cross. A cupola with four windows and four blind niches supported by pilasters sits on over the central part of the church. Matka Monastery church features the three-sided outside altar apse. The facades are enlivened with lesions while the windows are small and placed high in the walls providing larger space for frescoes. The frescoes date from the end of the 15th century and feature all the characteristics of the fresco painting during the Turkish period, represented in a considerable falling off in comparison with the nearby St. Andrew's frescoes. Five zones of frescoes are visible inside the church: full-length figures and medallions depict the Christ Passions and the Great Feasts scenes. Portraits of the patrons Milica and Nikola, dressed in bourgeois clothes are located in the floor level zone of the west wall. The painted monastic figures testify about the ancient monastic holy place, while frescoes of the Serbian saints *the Holy Simeon Nemanya and the St Peter of Korisha* confirm domination of the Pec Patriarchate during the reconstruction and fresco painting processes of the Holy Virgin Monastery in Matka canyon. The fresco painter did not have great skills and accomplished muddy color and uncertain drawing. Regarding the iconography details the painter frequently neglected the traditional sequence of the scenes.

Matka Monastery is a popular resort for the Skopje inhabitants and there is a small hotel nearby which is approached by an asphalt road. Existing monastery lodgings were erected in 1886. In 1998 the monastery was revived again. It is now a convent, at the head of which is the Abbess Perpetua. The Matka monastery complex today, besides the church, is comprised of mansion with the belfry, the Bishop's residence, the housekeeper's house and the monastery water tap with healthy and clean spring water.

The Jasen Forest Reserve was proclaimed the National Park in 1958. Jasen Forest Reserve covers an area of 24000 hectares and stretches across the mountain massifs of Suva Gora, Suva Planina and Karadzhica. This nature park of Macedonia belongs to the category of the Special Natural Reserves protecting many species of flora and fauna and other natural rarities.

Mavrovo National Park

The Mavrovo National Park is the largest protected area in the country making the largest National Park of Macedonia, close to the Macedonian border with Albania and Kosovo. Mavrovo National Park covers 11750 hectares, encompassing the most beautiful parts of western Macedonia the mountains of Bistra, Korab, South Šar Massifs, Dešat, *Radika River*, Mavrovo Lake and picturesque tiny villages of Mavrovi Anovi, Mavrovo, Leunovo, Nikiforovo, Galičnik, Rostuše, Gari, Janče, *Tresonče*, Bituše and *Lazaropole*, with total area of 73,088 hectares. Mavrovo was declared the National Park in 1949 to be enlarged in 1952 to 73100 hectares of which some 27000 hectares are forested. Relief of Mavrovo National Park is spectacularly diversified and encompasses 52 mountain peaks over 2000 meters ! Golem Korab Mountain which is 2764 meters high is the highest mountain peak of Macedonia and provides true hiking challenge, tourist attractions and stunning panorama and *other options of recreation*. Another mountainous range of the Mavrovo Municipality is Bistra Mountain with its most popular *Medeniza peak* (2.163 meters). The seat of the Mavrovo National Park lies in the village of Mavrovi Anovi on the very shore of Mavrovo Lake. From that point up to the peak of Korab Mountain and the very heart of the intact wilderness you need minimum 5 hours of rush walk along fragrant meadows full of flowers and from where beneficial smell of mint and other medicinal herbs spread all around.

The Mavrovo Ski Center named Zare Lazareski is an interesting and highly enjoyable and most popular ski resort of Macedonia. Its three chairlifts start from the doorstep of the area's hotels at an elevation of 1255 meters above sea level. Eleven more drag lifts bring the resorts capacity to a respectable 10.000 skiers an hour. The highest T-bar lift tops at 1860 meters. Large parts of the Mavrovo Ski resort are well protected from high winds and sheltered by the high hills of Korab Mountain, with the ski resort staying closed due to weather conditions only twice during the 2006 winter. Summer months in Mavrovo National Park are convenient for walking and mountaineering. The wide-spread pastures and clean spring water of the Mavrovo National Park are attractive for trekking trips, bivouacking, mountain biking and other kinds of recreation. It is presumed that Mavrovo National Park includes more than 1000 types of higher plant forms, of which about 100 are extremely rare and of Balkan endemic plants. Mavrovo National Park provides a sanctuary for bears, wolves, golden eagles and critically endangered species such as the balkan lynx, less than 50 of which are still thought to be alive. The main attraction is the chance to see and photograph wild Dinaric Pindus Brown Bear and potentially Lynx, Wolf, Boar, Deer and Goat species. Guests also take part in vital conservation work, including scientific surveys, tracking and the setting of camera traps.

The largest artificial lake in Macedonia is part of Mavrovo National Park. The Mavrovo Lake is 12 kilometers long and 3 kilometers wide and covers an area of 13,3 square km. On the southern side the Mavrovo Lake is surrounded with forested Vlainica Mountain, while in the north it borders with the Sarr Mountain. The coast of Mavrovo Lake is 24 kilometers long. The deepest measured spot of the Mavrovo Lake is 48 meters. Rich in famous lake trout, Mavrovo Lake is often visited by fishermen. Due to its elevation (1,220 meters), this mountainous lake sometimes freezes over in winter. Mavrovo Lake also makes an excellent swimming and boating spot in the summer months. An additional point of interest of Mavrovo Lake is the half-submerged *Saint Nicolas church* in the middle of it, built in 1850. The Saint Nicholas Church was built by builders from the Reka region from marble and granite. The Saint Nicholas church had marble iconostasis built by master zograph Dimitar Dičo Krstević. Locals of the Mavrovo area were telling that in construction of the Saint Nicholas church the most precious stone and special equipment was used. The Saint Nicholas church in Mavrovo Lake is one nave church with five sided apse, a bell towe and iconostasis. Icons were painted in 1855 by reputed icon painter Dičo Krstević, while later it was the icon painter Meletij Bojinov from Debar area who worked on the icons. The Serb benefactor Lady Bosiljka Janić erected the belfry in 1925 which is testified by the plaque dedicated to her husband Golub Janic, whose origins were from Mavrovo region. In law water level of the Mavrovo Lake, in the back part of the church one can see the tomb awith monument to the priest Jovan Milošević and his son Arsenije, erected in 1930.

One of the most impressive parts of the Mavrovo National Park is the stunning Radika River Gorge. On the heights of mountain slopes within and around the Mavrovo National Park there are 1*7 glacial lakes,* which make true mountainous landmarks of the site and excite their visitors.

Galičnik Wedding Festival is a feast celebrated by local Mijak population in the tiny village of Galičnik, within the Mavrovo National Park and winter and summer resort, at the altitude of 1350 meters, for the eyes and bliss for the soul, rich experience of many original and unforgettable wedding customs and rituals. Galičnik village is famous for its authentic countryside scenery and wonderful natural and unique architectural environment as it features well preserved traditional architecture, including an amphitheater in the village square. Saint Peter's Day is for centuries celebrated on the 12th July in the Galicnik village and it is the day of splendid traditional costumes, magnificent ceremonies and rituals of the unique *Galičnik wedding* whose wider significance comes to its crown by entering the treasury of spiritual values of humanity under UNESCO protection. Galichnik wedding comprises the most colorful wedding customs that represent a blend of Christian and pagan traditions which are performed with great attention to every detail, marking the three key moments in human life in all civilizations: birth, marriage, and death. Young men and women of Macedonia, born in Galičnik, ancient village in northwest Macedonia, have something that makes them very proud *an opportunity to wed in a traditional way, the way it was done in the past times in their village*. The mother-in-law ties an apron ("skutaca" or "futa") around the bride's waist and puts a white scarf on her head in order for the daughter-in-law to be a good housewife. Coins, wheat and candies are thrown from a sieve over the gathered guests; one bundle made of coins, wheat and candies is thrown on the roof tiles by the bride in order to be sweet, rich and happy. Two loaves of bread are put under the bride's armpits so everything would be a whole. The father-in-law puts a long woven cloth around the newly-wed couple and brings them over the doorstep into the house. Galičnik Wedding is an annual ritual, full of dancing and music of the *"zurla"* and "tapani" and numerous rituals buying the bride, shaving the bridegroom or rifle shooting... The Galičnik Wedding used to last for five days with its peak on the Saint Peter's Day, the 12th of July, the time of the year when couples would wed. Galičnik wedding in our time is part of the "Galičnik Summer", a two-day event taking place during the weekend closest to Saint Peter's Day.

Each year, the Galichnik wedding "candidates" participate in a competition resulting in one couple that gets the honor of having their wedding held in this small Macedonian village. The celebration starts off on Saturday and begins with the wedding, parade and dance, and lasts long into the night. The next day is reserved for traditional dances accompanied by hypnotic sounds of the tamburitza and the flute. Everyone is eager to see the men doing the dance called *"teskoto oro" (the hard one)*. The Teskoto Oro dance symbolizes the overcoming of life's difficulties. *Tesko oro* folk dance is very demanding because of the rhythm that continually accelerates while most of the dance is performed on one foot only. Waiting for the drums, the folk dance *"Svekrvino oro"* (Mother-in law's dance) is performed followed with taking the bride to the fountain, setting the wedding flag, inviting the dead, shaving the groom, taking the bride, kneading the bread, marriage ceremony in the church of SS Peter and Paul. A suggestive scenario, the Galichnik town architecture and its square make a perfect setting for men and women dressed in their traditional costumes; women in red, white, and black clothes. Men in linen trousers, waistcoats, ribbons, and hats that they exchange during the dance. The most important moment of Galičnik Wedding is the arrival of the bride and groom. Groom leads the white horse on whose back sits the bride. They come by the main road while girls walk in front of them throwing flowers and candy into the crowd. After that the girls join the other dancers of Galičnik Wedding and they dance until the late hours…. This is the memorable Galicnik Wedding !

Mijaci pl. Miyaks are the Serb tribe which settles the area of western part of the present North Macedonia in the course of the Radika River, the right tributary of Crni Drim River Black Drim River, that is known as the Reka region. Locals of the Reka region are known in other parts as Rekanci, but also Debarci for the fact that the nearest settlement is Debar, which they administratively belonged to during the Turkish rule. The term of Galičanci is also used after the once largest Miyak village of Galicnik. The Serbian tribe of Mijaks Miyaks in present north-western Macedonia in the Mala Dolna Reka known as 'Mijacija' is the Serb ethnic group which belongs to the old Balkan population, that for long time resisted Bulgarization and communist movement of Macedonization. Mijaks are organized in tribal communities similar to tribes in Herzegovina, Littoral, Old Crna Gora Old Montenegro, Brda Hills, Metohija and Raska areas. Mijaks are also very similar to the Serbs on the other side of the Sar Mountain, in the Sirinic Zhupa of Metohija area, around Strpce and Brezovica settlements in Kosovo and Metohija. The largest Macedonian settlements populated by Mijaks are Lazaropolje, Galicnik, Gari, Bituse, Selce, Osoj and Susica. However, today among Mijaks only minority declares themselves as Serbs, while majority declares them the Macedonians, and those who would consider themselves as Bulgarians almost do not exist.

It must be acknowledged that Galička svadba the Galičnik Wedding is an unique tourist attraction of Macedonia and the Balkans. However, unlike many other events, this one managed to preserve the atmosphere of an ancient and beautiful folk customs. The Galičnik wedding is the joy of the local people and visitors, worth experiencing along with amazing colors, dances, smells, flavors, rhythms, and the wonderful sun of the Macedonian summer.

Nidze Mountain Kajmakchalan

Nidze is mountain in south Macedonia, along which goes the border with Greece. The highest peak of the Nidze Mountain is Kajmakčalan, 2521 meters. Mountain Nidže had been created by fissure in Tertiary and comes in Paleosoic slate, while its highest parts feature some Mesosoic characteristics. Mountain Nidže is known by outstanding richness of forests, mountain pastures and diversified flora. Nidže Mountain spreads on the border between present Macedonia and Greece, east of the Pelagonija valley, and on the eastern slope it is almost precipitous, with so steep terrain that is almost impossible to climb. Towards northwest Nidže Mountain borders the Skočivir Ravine, while the Crna reka River /Black River/ joins in large bend with the Satoka River, which further flows in direction of more than 90 degrees southeast to its junction with the Gradashtanska River.

Despite centuries of dispute over who owns Macedonia, a part of the recently independent state of Macedonia remains of great historical significance to Serbs. During World War I, from 12th September until the 3rd October 1916, the Battle of Kajmakcalan between Serbian and Bulgarian-German troops took place at the Kajmakčalan and around the adjacent peaks, resulting in the great Serbian victory. Besides the strategic importance, Kajmakchalan peak was of the utmost importance for Serbs, as along its highest ranges spread the state border of the Kingdom of Serbia. Serbian solders were specially motivated to do what enemy considered impossible, and named the Kajmakchalan peak *"Gate of Serbia Vrata Srbije" or "Gate of freedom Kapija slobode"*.

Decision to break the Thessaloniki Salonica front was made in June 1918. The Serb Army was divided into two armies the First Army, commanded by Petar Bojovic, and the Second Army, led by Field Marshal Stepa Stepanovic, while Zivojin Misic was the Chief of General Staff of the Army. In his command to soldiers for breaking the Salonika Front, Zivojin Misic writes on 13 September 1918: „All commanders, brigadiers and soldiers must have the idea that the speed of progression in invasion would determine the success of the whole offensive. That speed is at the same time the best guarantee for surprise, as it gains enemy derangement and full freedom in our penetration actions. You should impudently penetrate, without rest, until the ultimate borders of human strength and horse endurance. To the death, do not stop ! Heroes, towards the Fatherland, with firm and steady faith and hope !" This command testifies on sturdiness and determination of the Serb people to liberate their homeland.

The Nidže mountain changed hands several times, but eventually the Bulgarian and German foes were driven back, and the Eastern Front saw a change in the course of the Great War. Yet nothing could prepare visitors for its breathtaking beauty, quietness and solitude, in contrast to the intolerable noise of the battle that raged there nearly 100 years ago. Valiant and heroic Serbian combat ended the bloodiest battle of the whole Salonica campaign with liberation of Bitola /Monastir/ within the Salonika front, and had marked the beginning of the successful outcome of the First World War. After the First World War, the chapel with the Memorial ossuary was erected on the Kamjakalan peak. There was carved inscription of the words of the Serbian King Aleksandar „*Mojim div junacima, neustrašivim i vernim, koji grudima svojim otvoriše vrata slobodi i ostadoše ovde, kao večni stanari na pragu otadžbine."* /*dedicated to my titan and fearless and faithful heroes who opened the door of freedom by their chests and remained here, as the eternal guardians on the foot of the homeland*/. Besides this ossuary, in the vicinity of the Kajmakcalan Mountain there are more graveyards of the Serbian solders, although the majority of killed solders were buried on the Zejtinlik graveyard in Thessaloniki.

The Serbs won the Kajmakcalan Battle, but they payed a very high price around 10.000 Serbian casualties and wounded. There is a tiny church dedicated to Saint Elijah Sveti Ilija made up of weapons, shells and barbed wire fence off the church, in a testament to eternal peace and a crypt for the Serbian soldiers who heroically died in the Kajmakchalan battle. In the ossuary beneath the church there are bones and remains of 4600 Serbian heroic solders who built in their lives into the break of the Thessaloniki Front, and the triumphal end of the Great War. On the Nidze Mountain, in the foot of the Kajmakchalan peak, there are 44 Serbian small military cemeteries. In the church of Saint Elijah there is an urn which contains the heart of Dr. Archibald Reiss, the Swiss-German father of Forensic Medicine, who sought to bring to the *world's attention the slaughter of Serbian civilians during the Great War*. It says :

"In this urn, On Kajmakčalan's peak, The golden heart sleeps, Of a Serbian friend, 8th August 1929".

Such was Reiss's loyalty to the Serbian cause that he fought alongside Serbs, lived in Belgrade until his death, and declared in his will that his heart be embalmed and placed in an urn on Kajmakčalan. This unique testament to the indescribably heroic Serbian history and numerous Serbian victims at the Thessaloniki-Salonica Front is not that well known, and deserves not to remain so, but to gain constant admiration of the world as the legacy of Serbs among the present mountains of Macedonia.

Veternik Mountain is part of the Kajmakcalan mountain masif. In memory and respect for the Serbian volunteers of the Firt World War, in 1923 was founded a settlement of Veternik in Novi Sad for army veterans and invalids who fought on the Veternik Mountain in Macedonia. After the First World War King Aleksandar granted land in Novi Sad to his brave soldiers who were permanently blinded by the nerv gas in fierce battles against the Bulgarians on the Veternik Mountain. The then Veternik had only two streets, with typical houses erected on granted estates, of which some are still preserved. It was 37 families of the brave Salonica soldiers with 107 members of their families who settled the fertile Vojvodina plain and created a nucleus of the present Veternik settlement in Novi Sad.

Ohrid

Ohrid is the marvelous city in the beautiful south-western part of Macedonia, with some 42000 inhabitants, and also leading summer tourist center of the country which is often considered as the "Balkan soul" and the cradle of the Slavic literacy. The town of Ohrid, situated on the shore of Ohrid Lake, some 170 km south-west of Skopje the Macedonian capital, features outstanding natural beauties, historical and cultural heritage, and since 1979 enjoys the protection of UNESCO. The wonderful Ohrid Lake covers picturesque area of about 350 sq km and is known for its crystal clear water, which is visible down to 22 meters, of a total maximum depth of 286 meters. The astonishingly clean and clear waters of the Ohrid Lake, together with the serene stillness of its mountain settings have captivated visitors since prehistoric times. Above the valley of Ohrid lake rises Mount Galičica with the Galičica National Park, recognized by the International Union for Conservation of Nature (IUCN) as an extremely important region and protected by law since 1958. Thanks to the several hundred original rarities and the protected plant and animal species, Galičica has been internationally recognized as an Important Plant Area, a Primary Butterfly Area, as well as an Emerald Site (future part of the European Natura 2000 network). Because of the extraordinary biodiversity and the international significance, in 2014 Galičica National Park became part of the UNESCO World Network of Biosphere Reserves.

Wanderlust named Ohrid Lake as one of the most incredible lakes in the world. While the Ohrid lake is filled up by water from three rivers, most of Ohrid's water comes from another lake *Prespa Lake* which is located on the other side of Galicica Mountain-National Park. Due to the high elevation, Prespa Lake spills its water down to Ohrid through mountain springs, the most important ones being Ostrovo and Biljana, located the Saint Naum Monastery and Ohrid town.

With its ancient necropolis, fortress, amphitheaters, baths, arenas, parts of villas, temples and Byzantine basilicas, Ohrid is considered as *one of the most ancient towns in the Balkans*, a living testimony of the cultural competition of the civilizations and the everlasting mark of their residence in the area. Ohrid abounds with a large number of archaeological sites dating from the Neolithic, antique and medieval periods, as well as numerous early Christian and Medieval Churches with marvelous mosaics, frescoes and icons, lovely beaches, and variety of accommodation facilities. The Ohrid Samuil's Fortress Samoilova Tvrdina is one of the most popular destinaion in Ohrid, built in the 10th century during the reign of Tsar Samuil of Ohrid, which was the political and ecclesiastical capital of the first Bulgarian Empire (681–1018). Through history Ohrid was such an important religious settlement that it was claimed to had 365 churches one church for every day of the year.

Name of Ohrid comes from its location built "on a hill" /"*vo hrid*"/. The whole old town of Ohrid is surrounded by walls and is crowned by the King Samoil's Citadel. Ohrid Fortress is considered to be the oldest and best-preserved fortress in Macedonia. The ancient Ohrid is built in the shape of amphitheater with numerous tiny traditional houses looking towards the lake. Those interesting houses of Ohrid were built in past centuries in genuine Oriental style of building authentic Balkan architecture characterized by the beautiful balconies and houses with upper floors more spacious than the ground floor. The old part of Ohrid includes impressive *bazaar with market, fountain, hammam and numerous handcraft workshops and various tiny shops and workshops that sell unique handwork items /Ohridski biser, jewelry, leather products, sweets, wood-carved items, Byzantine painting workshop and old Macedonian musical instruments and the famous Macedonian embroidery, outstanding Macedonian music CD…../* and take you back to the past Oriental times. The famous Ohrid pearls are made with usage of the scales of the endemic Ohrid Lake Plasica fish which makes them the unique in the world. Ohrid pearl is probably the best souvenir from Ohrid, as well as the most appropriate gift for a lady. Risteski Family in Ohrid is one of the original pearl-making families here, handcrafting and selling Ohrid pearls of the finest quality. "It might be because of the pleasant climate, or the lake, or the strong fort of Samuil, or for the flat and fruitful field, that have attracted blacksmiths, woodcarvers and craftsman of all arts and masters to make miracles in wood, stone, silver, copper and gold to settle here". Camil Sijaric

Icons of the Ohrid Icon Gallery comprising period of almost a millennium, from the middle of the 11th till the end of the 19th century are a remarkable and an indivisible segment of the rich cultural and historical heritage of Ohrid, the city where the Slavic literacy and culture have sprouted. Created in the Constantinople and Salonika icon workshops, or in the local icon workshops in Ohrid, these icons have been an inseparable part of the iconostasis in the churches they have been ordered and painted for and some of them best accomplishments of the Byzantine icon painting in whole. The Icon of Jesus Christ, dimension of 135 x 93 cm is kept, among the other precious art works, in the Gallery of Icons in Ohrid, set in the complex of the Holy Virgin of Peribleptos. Ohrid and the gorgeous Macedonia is our favorite destination of unrepeatable beauty.

Ohrid attractions and Places to see : Tzar Samuil's Fortress, Antique Theater, Episcopal Basilica, St Clement's Church of St Panteleimon at Plaosnik, Cathedral of St Sophia, Holy Mother of God Peribleptos Church Holy Mother of God Peribleptos Church, Sveti Jovan Kameno Saint John Theologian Kaneo Church, Saint Naum Monastery, Cave church, Icon Gallery, Velestovo, Vevcani and Trpejca villages...

Monastery of Saint Pantelejmon Ohrid

The Monastery of Saint Panteleimon, the protector of health is one of the oldest Slavic monasteries in the Balkans and the oldest Slavic monument of culture. With the construction of St. Panteleimon in Ohrid by Clement (893), downhill from Ohrid fortress, the Macedonian Slavs gained not only their first great religious and educational center but also the conditions necessary to develop their aesthetic feelings, accepting and continuing existing artistic forms but expanding into new directions as well. For example, Clement used a ruined three-conchae church for the foundation of St. Panteleimon, added some original parts, and obtaining thereby new "oval" forms. Saint Panteleimon Monastery had an extremely important role in the education of the Macedonians during the period of strong influence of the Byzantine Empire. The Saint Panteleimon Monastery stands on a hill overlooking the Ohrid Lake, which is today known as Plaošnik. Remains of the early-christian basilica were found on the old cult place above which the small three-nave church was erected in the 7th century. Saint Clement of Ohrid rebuilt the church and used it as a liturgical building and place for teaching his disciples his variation of the Glagolithic alphabet, known as the Cyrillic alphabet. Clement personally built a crypt inside the Saint Panteleimon Monastery in which he was buried after his death in 916, his tomb still exists today.

Many archaeologists believe that Clement himself designed and constructed the Saint Panteleimon Monastery. Clement, along with Naum of Preslav would use the monastery as a basis for teaching the Glagollithic and Cyrillic alphabets to the Christian Slavs thus making it a university. Clement built his monastery on a restored church and a Roman Basilica of five parts (the remains of the basilicas can still be seen outside the monastery). Judging by the architectural style and design of the monastery, researchers say that Saint Clement intended for his building to be the literary school for disciples, thus it is believed to be the first and oldest discontinued university in Europe. The common themes for fresco paintings in Saint Panteleimon, Ohrid are "Birth of Mother God", "Transfiguration", "The Entry into Jerusalem", "Descent from the Cross" etc. Among the paintings in the Monastery of Saint Panteleimon, the fresco of *"The Lamentation of Christ"* is fascinating. This painting is considered to be a masterpiece by many art historians. The exterior of the monastery contains a large number of finely detailed mosaics not far from a stone Baptismal font used to baptize his disciples.

Saint Sophia Cathedral Ohrid

St. Sophia Church is one of the most impressive medieval buildings in Ohrid and a unique work of architecture of the Byzantine region. St Sophia is a large three-nave cathedral with a dome at the center, built on the foundations of an old cult during the period of the Tzar Samuel. In the 11th century the Saint Sophia basilica in Ohrid was thoroughly renovated when it was fresco decorated. In 1317, during the Serbian rule, the monumental exo-narthex with its open galleries and two towers ending in small domes, a rare architectural accomplishment both in Macedonia and the world in general, was added to the Church of St. Sophia in 1317, what greatly contributed to the beauty of Saint Sophia Church. During the Ottoman era Saint Sophia Church in Ohrid was converted into a mosque. Frescoes of Saint Sophia Cathedral are considered the best preserved Byzantine paintings. The frescoes in the Saint Sophia Cathedral are characterized by the postures of the figures and the archaic forms, united in an artistic and iconographic whole unique to church painting of the time. The best preserved frescoes of St Sophia Cathedral in Ohrid are in the altar with the Holy Virgin on the throne holding little Christ in her arms. Six angels are kneeling towards the Holy Virgin approaching her from the southern and the northern wall. Beneath the Holy Virgin fresco there is *"Communion of apostles"* scene which is one of the most interesting fresco of the St Sophia Church. Among depicted portraits of numerous saints and patriarchs in Saint Sophia Cathedral, there are portraits of brothers Cyril and Methodius, the first Slavic missioners and founders of the First Slavic University and St Clement of Ohrid, their disciple. Since its builders blessed it with wonderful acoustics, the Cathedral of Saint Sophia and its front garden are the main stage of the annual *Ohrid Summer Festival.*

Osogovo Mountains

Osogovo Mountain is the splendor of the eastern Macedonia and a pure ecosystem containing the mountainous crystal waters, green forests, rocky ridges, lakes, deer, wild strawberries ... The Osogovo region disposes with rich archaeological deposits, churches, monasteries, rural places with specific ethnology, folklore customs and recognizable rich traditional kitchen. Various valuable herbs, featuring ingredients hard to find and inexpensive, hand-picked on the high pastures that adorn the tops of the Osogovski mountains, on the border with Bulgaria, are found from early spring until late summer, such are peppers (spicy or not), rosemary, basil, peppermint, wild mint, and thyme, as well as some little known autonomous species. The Mt. Orbelos, Orbelus was identified to correspond with the mountain Osogovo in Republic of Macedonia. The Orbelus Mountain forms a part of a great chain separating Paeonia from Dardania and Moesia (Strab. Epit. VII. P. 329.). The area of the Osogovoro Mountain is rich in ore deposits and mines (gold, silver, copper, lead....), which had attracted Saxons in the 13th century, who have settled those regions in order to restore exploit of the mineral wealth.

The climbers will surely be challenged by the Osogovo peaks of *Ruen* (2252 m) and *Carev Vrv* (2085 m), while the *Ponikva* tourist center, at the altitude of 1560 meters is recommended for real nature enthusiasts, who would enjoy the comforts of civilization. Those who enjoy traditional ambiance within the intact nature will surely enjoy the atmosphere in the village of Polaki, a place where, among the stone houses, time has lost its meaning. Near the village one can find the hunting ground Polaki and enjoy trophy hunting or photo-safari. The Osogovo Mountain range is a real challenge for many mountain bikers and off-road adventurers. The numerous rivers and lakes make trip to the Osogovo Mountains an unforgettable adventure. In the heart of Osogovo Mountains there are also the *Monastery of St. Spas Saint Savior Monastery* and one of the most beautiful monasteries in the Balkans *St. Joachim of Osogovo Monastery.*

Pelister National Park

Pelister National Park is the oldest among national parks of Macedonia which obtained this status in 1948. Pelister National Park is located on northern part of the Baba Mountain in the south-western Macedonia, above the eastern shores of the Prespa Lake, and west of Pelagonija plain, only 7 km away from the city of Bitola. Pelister National Park covers 12500 hectares of the mountain slopes of Baba Mountain at the elevation from 700 to 2600 meters. Baba Mountain stretches direction north-south and makes the natural border between the Bitola Field on east and the Resen Field and the Prespa Lake on the west, spreading its southern part into Greece.

There are many mountain peaks in Pelister National Park higher than 2000 meters of which *Pelister* /2601 meters/ is the highest. Two stunning glacial lakes of the Pelister National Park, *the Big and the Small Lake* are especially attractive and called the *Pelister Mountainous Eyes*. The Big Lake of Pelister Mountain-National Park is set at the altitude of 2218 meters which is one of the highest lakes of Macedonia. Vast panorama from Pelister National Park spreads to the Jakupica Mountain in the north, and to the Selecka Planina Mt and Kajmakcalan peak on the east, and to the Prespa Lake, and the Galicica and Jablanica Mountains to the northwest. From Pelister one can observe the Pelagonija Plain and enjoy the colors of the Prespa Lake.

Flora and fauna of Pelister National Park are rich and diverse with lots of endemic plants and wild animals. The most important among the floral species of Pelister National Park is the *molika pine /Pinus peuce/*, the autochthonous species of the pine from the tertiary age which can live up to 300 years.

The Pelister features great historical trails dating from the First World War, with reconstructed trenches, bridges and cannon positions, which presents the remembrance of the Battle of Monastir in 1917 during the Salonika /Thessaloniki/ Campaign in World War I. Visitors have lecture "in open" about the Pelister as a very important war and battle field during the First World War, especially at the end of 1916 and beginning of 1917, when both sides of the Central Powers and Entente suffered great losses. The local inhabitants have experienced the most immense agonies with up to thousands shells a day, which were fired on the town of Bitola from the positions on Pelister.

The village of Brajchino is situated 6 km from Lake Prespa in a valley of the foot of Baba Mountain, on the edge of Pelister's National Park and represents the center of ecotourism of Prespa region. This authentic Macedonian village has maintained its traditional character and an intimate link with its surroundings, which emphasized its "eco" label and had made it became part of the tourist map of the world. Brajchino is a mountain village (at an altitude of about 1000 m above sea level) disturbed only by the roaring sound of the local river and by the evening winds rustling through the trees. It features richness of sparkling springs, dewy and green forests, breathtaking mountain peaks, apples grown at the altitude higher than 1000 meters and outstandingly flavorful strawberries matured at the end of summer. Occasionally you may hear a dog barking, a cock crowing or a cow-bell ringing. The village has about 150 inhabitants and 100 houses. Cattle breeding was a main activity in the past, but has been replaced by agriculture, especially fruit growing. Many families from Brajchino, emigrated to Canada, U.S.A, Australia, and the Scandinavian countries in the middle of the 20th century.

Hidden in the foot of Baba Mountain, while freshened by the clear breeze coming from Pelister Mountain from one side and bathed by benefiting Prespa sun, this village of authentic architecture and warm locals /of those who remained here, since majority had left to overseas countries/ is unique and memorable in terms of its location and natural ambiance. Those benefits are recognized by number of tourists from all over the world who come here to learn "the synthesis of men and culture and nature" while enjoying numerous privileges of small and serene community, where hosts take care of visitors as their own family. Direct contact with the local people and their hospitality makes your stay in Brajchino a unique experience. The people of Brajchino still produce a variety of food for themselves or to sell at the market place: garden vegetables; meat and dairy products from their livestock; honey; apples from their orchards; mushrooms, herbs, and berries from the forest; and fish from the river and from Lake Prespa.

Brajchino is a perfect location for combing outdoor activities on the mountain, with the leisure of the lake. The Mountain Nature Trail is the main natural attraction, leading from the village of Brajchino to Golemo Ezero (glacial "Big Lake"). The trail links the Lake Prespa region with the National Park of Pelister and provides breathtaking views, magnificent landscapes and rare species. Hiking time through

Pelister National Park takes approximately 5 -7 hours and mountain guides are a must for hikers not familiar with the region. They will also enhance your experience in the mountains with their knowledge of local wildlife which includes bears, wolves, boars, etc. Ursus arctos the Macedonia's brown bear population appears to be a key link in the distribution of one of Europe's largest brown bear populations, the Dinaric-Pindos population. Even earlier the brown bear had prime role e.g. in middle ages it was what lion was in the antiquity, a forest king that got the main mythological pedestal in the local culture.

Prespa Lake Prespa Region

Prespa Lakes region is the trans-boundary park of the Balkans and ecosystem of great significance thanks to its biodiversity and endemic species in the Balkans and north-western corner of Greece, at 850 meters above sea level, surrounded with mountain massifs, shared between Greece, Albania and Macedonia. Prespa region hosts more than 1,500 species of plants, 40 species of mammals, 260 of migratory and non-migratory birds, 32 reptiles and amphibians, and 17 species of fish including a number of species found only here. The wetlands of Prespa *are a bird-watchers paradise* between the Resen field and Baba, Suva Gora and Galicica mountains. The surrounding mountains of Prespa area make it one of the *last European homes of brown bears, wolves, chamois and wild boar* whilst the lake host breeding colonies of Dalmatian and White Pelicans as well as pygmy cormorants.

Prespa Lake covers an area of 294 sq km, with a maximum depth of 54 meters. Prespa Lakes lie in a tectonic valley between the mountains of *Baba on the east (2601m), Galichica (2288m) and Petrino on the west and Suva Gora Mountain (1857m) on the south*. Galicica Mountains-National Park separates Lake Megali Prespa from Ohrid Lake which are connected to Ohrid Lake via underground karstic channels. Prespa lake is set at the altitude that is 150 meters higher that the altitude of Ohrid lake so the water from Prespa Lake keeps pouring into Ohrid lake. Famous Biljana's springs in Ohrid are actually the place where Prespa lake comes out of mountain Galičica and falls into Ohrid lake. The mountains surrounding the Prespa lakes are often over 2000 meters high, and offer marvelous views to the lake blueness with scattered settlements on the shores where live extremely hospitable and diligent locals in old stone houses with mud parts. There are few fantastic authentic restaurants and accommodation facilities in traditional stone houses to host visitors keen to explore those immense beauties, attractions and lifestyle. Bike and hike tours in the Prespa region provide visitors the chance to enjoy landscapes filled with picturesque villages, marvelous lakes with waters so pure that they are almost transparent surrounded by majestic snowy mountain tops. The smell of herbs on the mountain meadows calm all the senses, already cleared by the fresh air and the spring waters.

The two Prespa Lakes Golema (Great Island, Macro Prespa on the Macedonian side of the Prespa Lake) and Malo (Small Island, Mikri Prespa on the Albanian side of the Prespa Lake) are connected one with another by only a narrow strip of dry land and are the *only lakes on the Balkan Peninsula to have islands*. The five islands *Golem Grad, Mali Grad, Pirg, Agios Achillaeos and Vidrinec* are located in the magically beautiful Prespa Region junction of three countries that share the lakes of Prespa today *Macedonia, Albania and Greece*. The Mali grad Island belongs to the Albanian part of the Prespa Lake and hosts the Holy Virgin church erected in the second half of the 14th century. Its khtetor was the Serbian nobleman *Novak Mrasorović* who was vassal of the King Vukašin Mrnjavčević. In the interior of the Holy Virgin Church there are frescoes and inscriptions which help us date the church in the period around 1369. On the western facade is painted the composition of donors-khtetors which depicts the nobleman Novak, his wide Kali and their children.

The Golem Grad is non-populated island in Prespa Lake, about 18 hectares big and includes ancient ruins from the Neolithic, Roman, Hellenic, Byzantine and Ottoman times. Prespa region featured during its long history a very important geostrategic position. During the existence of the Roman Empire, some very significant roads, such as the Via Egnatia, passed through Prespa region and made it a popular trading center. Along this monumentally long Roman road, many settlements and villages were built. Because of its good position and great importance, Prespa was made the capital during the reign of Tsar Samoil in the 10th century who built the Basilica of Agios Achillios Saint Achilles and the magnificent residence, on the island of same name with intention to be buried in its atrium. The Basilica of Agios Achilleios was built after 983 or 986 by Tsar Samuel of the Bulgars in order to house the relics of Saint Achilleios, bishop of Larissa, which the Bulgarian troops had brought after their conquest of the city. The Saint Achilles church was founded as an Episcopal church, housing the See of the Bulgarian Patriarch for a short time, after his transfer from Edessa. It was on the island of Agios Achilleos in Mikri Prespa where in the 11th century the family of Tsar Samuel surrendered to the Byzantine Emperor Basil II and the Bulgarian Empire ceased to exist. After the restoration of Byzantine rule to the area, from 1018 and on, the Saint Achilles church continued as a bishopric until the first decades of the 15th century when it was abandoned. This seemingly remote area was part of the Bulgarian Empire in the 10th century, when some of these churches were first built. But most belong to the period after 1018 when Emperor Basil II reconquered the region, whereupon it became a favorable stopping-point for travelers traversing the Balkans from the Adriatic Sea to Constantinople.

One of the most famous cultural and historical monuments in all the Balkans from the Byzantine period is the *Church of Saint George* built and wonderfully fresco-painted in the 12th century in the Kurbinovo village. However there are many other churches. monasteries and hermitages of Prespa region interesting to visit too: the 11th century church of Agios Germanos with its beautiful frescoes, the recently restored 15th century church of Agios Nikolaos on the edge of Pili village, or the church of the Virgin of the Porphyra on the island of Agios Achillios, Agios Athanasios,... There are 130 archaeological localities registered in the Prespa region from various periods of the development of material culture, about 1000 archaeological exhibits, 500 coins and 450 exhibits of the ethnological inheritance. During the Medieval period there was a monastery complex on the island with the Churches of St Peter, St Demetrius and Vlaia.

Brsjaci pl. Brsyaks Brsjac tribe make one of five ancient Serb tribes of the Macedonian Slavs to which belonged the *Holy King Jovan Vladimir Drvenarovic, the first Serbian Holy Martyr*. This old Serb tribe appeared in Thessaloniki at the beginning of the 7th century, and is recorded to have existed in the areas between Ohrid and Veles in present Macedonia. Sons of the Brsjac prince Nikola David, Moses, Aron and Samuil were leaders of the uprising against Byzantium, and have created and established the first state of the Macedonian Slavs. „Samuilo tsar of the Macedonian Slavs, 976-1014, son of the Brsiac prince Nikola, together with his brothers led uprising in Macedonia, against Byzantium which was ruled by the Tsar Basil II, and have created the first Macedonian state with the seat in Prespa and Ohrid. After defeat of Bulgaria in battles with Byzantium, he enlarged borders of his state up to the Sava and the

Danube rivers in the northwest, and to the Black Sea in the east, including states of Zeta, Raska and the northern Bulgaria.

On the 13th June 2013 the Albanian part of the Prespa, covering an area of 15.100 ha was added to the list of Wetlands of International Importance under the *Ramsar Convention,* while the part of the Prespa Lake which belongs to the FYR of Macedonia (18,920 ha) has been on the Ramsar list since 1995. Prespa Lake is one of the three largest lakes on the Balkan Peninsula.

Prespa region is the biggest and the most successful *apple producer* in the Balkans. The apples produced in this region are characterized by their *high quality and they are specifically juicy*. Like in almost all corners of the Balkans, red peppers are feature of the Prespa region, hanging in bundles out in the sun to dry and imbuing the autumnal neighborhood with the smells and colors of summer. Peppers contain a natural relaxant which helps to reduce anxiety or depression and to alleviate insomnia. The red peppers of the shores of Prespa Lake with their rich flesh and taste make the basis of much of the irresistible mouth-watering dishes of the region. The uniquely friendly residents of the Prespa region really understand a little secret about peppers red, green, yellow, blazing and aromatic which need to be roasted or fried to truly reveal their sumptuous flavor. The red peppers of Prespa region evoke the past times when grandmothers sat in front of the stove, patiently cleaning roasted peppers, the calluses on their hands softened by oil and their souls sweetened by redolent aroma.... It is strongly believed that today in Macedonia one can enjoy the unique flavor of the red peppers with thousand ways of cooking it !

Prespa Lake has also become attractive to visitors for its island tourism. The coast of the western part of the beautiful Prespa lake is full of cliffs, while in the eastern part dominate beautiful sandy beaches. The water of the Prespa lake has it's highest temperature in August, 24,3 degrees C, while in winter is the coldest and sometimes may freeze. The color of the Prespa lake water is variable yellow-green and heavenly blue. There are number of walking and trekking visitors who take the gravel roads and mountain paths to explore abandoned villages, historical monuments or the rich flora and fauna of the Prespa Lakes area. Various water-based activities are available on Great Prespa Lake: fishermen take visitors on boat tours from the village of Psarades, while swimming, canoe, kayak and rowing can be enjoyed at the beach of Koula in the summer. Golem Grad Island of the Prespa Lake, which is the only island in Macedonia, is a rare natural phenomenon and a real natural treasure. The Prespa region is ecologically speaking the cleanest part of Macedonia, its nature seemingly untouched by human hands. Boat trips are organized around the island and land trips under the auspices of the Galichica National Park. The Prespa water temperature in summer ranges from 18 to 24° C. The white Dalmatian pelican, black raven, heron and gull all congregate near the lake so abundant with fish, which include varieties such as trout, carp, red finned carp, chub, barbell, and others. Brown Bears live in the mountains surrounding the Prespa Lake. The beauty of the Prespa Lakes landscape, picturesque sleepy villages and the rich cultural heritage mostly from the Byzantine and Ottoman eras provide an added attraction for visitors. With its irregular coastline, plethora of bays, extraordinary cleanliness of water, pristine nature, and setting between three national parks, Prespa Lakes are truly places one must visit.

Prilep

Prilep is the second largest city in Pelagonia the largest and outstandingly fertile plain /granary/ in North Macedonia. Prilep is the fourth largest town of North Macedonia situated in the north-eastern part of Pelagonija plain /south-central part of North

Macedonia/, at altitude of 620 meters and gifted with extraordinary heritage and nature. Prilep is traditional trading center, but also center for production of *high-quality tobacco* and cigarettes and the metal processing, electronic, timber, textiles, and food industries. Many of the world's largest cigarette makers use extraordinary Prilep's tobacco in their cigarettes after it is processed in local factories. Finest Prilep tobacco is dried everywhere on the streets of Prilep and in front of the houses. *Prilep influenced the whole Macedonia not only by characteristics of its civil population, but also by its historical features connected mostly with the hometown of Marko Kraljevic, but also by its trading tradition.*

Prilep abounds in historical monuments which inspire fascinating tales of its past trat generate attractive cultural and sports events to attend all year round. The *Old Bazaar in Prilep* is an urban complex that had its biggest growth in the second half of the 18th and early 19th century, when Prilep was developed and prosperous trade and craft center. In the second half of the 19th century, after a series of fires that affected the Old Bazaar in 1854, in 1866 and 1873, the economic and trade power of Prilep declines. The Old Bazaar of Prilep gets today's look in the second half of the 19th and first half of the 20th century *the Clock Tower, the Kurshumli Han, House of Bekteshovci, the Turkish bath of Chifte Hammam, the Charshi Mosque* built during the rule of the sultan Mehmed the Second Conqueror, the Varos area with numerous monasteries, cultural sites and monuments....

The Ali Čair is the settlement dating from the Neolithic and Roman period of history. Remains of the ancient city of Stibera, which date from the 4th-3rd century BC are set 16 km west of Prilep, in the Chepigovo village, by the confluence of the Blato river with the Crna Reka River. The ancient itineraria records the fact that *Styberra* is situated by the road *Stobi-Heraclea*. At the Stibera site were discovered 28 monuments with inscriptions and names of deities and donors, and 27 monuments of the ancient cult statues and portraits. Among the finds of the cult statues there are gods of Asclepius, Hermes and Bachus, and female statues and imperial statues of the Stibera inhabitants. *National museum of Prilep* was and is the holder of numerous scientific research and conservation projects, organizer of many exhibitions and cultural events and a nursery of experts participating in the implementation of various projects in Macedonia, the former Yugoslavia, but also in European countries especially those who developed the Slavic archaeology.

During the 14th century Prilep was one of the capitals of the Serbian Empire during the reign of Tsar Dusan and center of later Lordship of Serbian king Marko Mrnjavčević. Prilep came into Serbian hands sometime in 1334 when Emperor Dusan captured it from the Byzantine Emperor Andronicus III. They signed a peace treaty, retaining the city to Dusan, where he resided in 1348. Charter of Emperor Dusan issued to Saint Sava's cell on Mount Athos speaks of 'the greatly famed city of Prilep'. It was the time when Emperor Dusan made Prilep one of his capitals, building himself an imperial palace and establishing his court and administration there. In 1350 or earlier, Dusan awarded Prilep and its hinterland to Vukasin who had himself crowned king in 1365. When his father was killed in the Battle of Maritza in 1371, Marko succeeded to his titles and was allowed by the Ottomans to continue ruling from Prilep by paying tribute to the sultan.

The Medieval town of Prilep was at the foothill of the rocky Varosh area, known as the Markovi kuli the towers of Marko, built on the place of the Roman settlement of *Ceramiae*. The Varosh complex in Prilep resembles the 'eagle's nest' among the magnificent rocks, on the south-western side of the Markovi kuli the Marko's towers which is rocky mass composed of numerous, diverse small denudation forms representing exceptionally fine sculpture of the relief. Such an intensive concentration and such diversity of micro relief forms as at Markovi Kuli have not been recorded so far in broader environment. Mining and trade have flourished in Medieval Serbian states in the 14th and the 15th centuries and during that period domestic and foreign master goldsmiths manufactured and produced a large number of finest pieces of jewelry, especially rings, creating the special *Serbian style of the jewelry patterns called "Serbian way"* in those times, which was very reputable even outside of Serbia. That style was mixture of Byzantine and Western European patterns modified by the local tradition. Large number of preserved jewelry pieces shows large typological diversity and use of precious materials and highly developed and advanced techniques of ornamentation.

The Varosh Monastery complex in Prilep includes foundations of necropolis and settlements from the Bronze and Iron ages, thermal spas from the Roman period and numerous well preserved cultural-historical monuments from the Middles ages. Varosh area dates from the ancient history, built for defensive purposes, but it persisted through the Medieval period, and may have been the key residential and economic site at Prilep in the 14th century. The remains of preserved Medieval Varosh churches undoubtedly prove the intense spiritual life that evolved in the Middle Ages, said to have had 77 churches at the end of the 18th century of which 7 survived in the 19th century. In the 14th century the King Marko Mrnjavcevic built upon this a defensive stronghold. After death of King Marko, in the Rovina Battle in 1395, the town of Prilep was conquered by the Ottomans, who built the town we see today, whose remains are pretty well preserved.

Treskavec Monastery built in the 14th century, set in the beautiful bare scenery. Thanks to its unique position above and within the rocky surroundings the Treskavec Monastery is renowned as the place with the most beautiful sunset in Macedonia. The frescoes inside of the Treskavac church are in pretty good condition and date from different periods of the 14th, 15th, 16th and 19th centuries. Specially interesting is woodcarving of the door and other furniture in the church. The monks that live here are quiet and keep to themselves. The hike to the Treskavec Monastery takes at least 2 hours, but it is through fascinating scenery. If you go in summer start early, if you want to take the hike in winter, early spring or late fall, ask around before to make sure the path is passable.

In ancient period the cult of Draconus deity spread in the area of Prilep and its surroundings, which surely was part of the Asclepius cult. It is depicted by two snakes rising from both sides of an egg. Prilep has been mentioned for the first time in the historical records in 1014. The territory of the city and its countryside were one of the most important strategical, political and military places in this part of the Balkans, as many important crossroads, which led from Greece to Adriatic see, were crossing Pelagonija Plain. The important antique roads "Via Egnazia" and "Via Militaris" had its most natural connection with the whole Balkans, crossing Prilep. The shortest road that connects Venetia and Dubrovnik business people with the ones in Thessaloniki was crossing Prilep, too. Through the centuries many cultures flourished on this space, like Hellenic, Roman, Byzantine, Slavic culture and others too. The most representative monumental complexes from the antique period testify about the rich history of Prilep : Bedem in Cepigovo walls, Bezisten between Prilepec and Volkovo, Stibera, Alcomena, Keramia, Colobansa and some places in the city.

Prilep, the seat of the Prince Marko Kraljevic, legendary person of the epic poetry, keeps significant remains of the medieval fortification. As per Byzantine architectural principles in the Byzantine world, the strong walls, strengthen with rectangular towers have been built on the rocky reef. The most significant personality of the Serbian epic poetry Marko Kraljevic /Prince Marko Mrnjavcevic/ made Prilep, his hometown, renown by his outsanding valiant reputation. Marko Mrnjevčević, know as Kraljević Marko Prince Marko was the Serbian nobleman who ruled the area around Prilep from 1371 til 1395, During time Marko Kraljević raised into the mythological personality and became the national hero in the epic poetry and novels of Bulgarians, Serbs, Macedonians, Croats, Montenegrin and Romanians. Epic poets of the Balkans have created the myth of extremely strong and brave man Marko Kraljevic.

Markovi Kuli The Fortress (Towers) of King Marko: Marko's towers, are included among the five strongest and most unconquerable fortresses in the Balkans. Markovi kuli site is situated to the northwest of Prilep, just above the village of Varoš. The towers of Serbian medieval Prince Marko Mrnjavčević are located on a 120-180 meters high hill, surrounded by steep slopes covered with minute granite stones. The upper part of the former settlement can be reached from its north and south side. The rampart on this terrain dates from the 13th and 14th centuries and is in good condition. The walls are about one meter thick and were built of limestone mortar and rest upon the large limestone rocks. According to some historical findings, until the second part of the 14th century and even later, this fortress was defended by only 40 soldiers.

Markovi kuli in Prilep were named after the last king Marko, but the studies say that it was actually a much older fortress, originating from the 4th century and the 3rd century BC. Archaeological excavations revealed the traces of several epochs from the necropolis of the early iron period, to remains of the ancient population and of the late middle ages. The fortress consists of four defensive areas. Today, it present a symbol of Prilep.

In folk tradition, are mentioned the chapel dedicated to Saint Luke, while in the charter of King Dusan, along with the Treskavec

Monastery are also listed several churches : *St. John the Baptist, St. George, Sveti Vrachi /Holy Healers/, St. Theodore and St. Demetrius.* From the number of churches built in the Varosh area, today are preserved: Saint Nicholas /Sveti Nikola, built in 1299/, Monastery of St. Archangel Michael /Manastir Sveti Arhangel Mihajlo/, St. Demetrius /Sveti Dimitrije/, St. Athanasius /Sveti Atanasije/, Saints Peter and Paul /Sveti Petar i Pavle/ and chuch of the Holy Virgin /Sveta Bogorodica/.

Mound of the Unbeaten Mogila is a World War II Memorial in the Park of the Revolution in Prilep. The unique anti fascist monument and memorial complex were built of white marble by the famous Yugoslav sculptor Bogdan Bogdanovic in 1961 in honor to the martyrs and fallen anti-fascist fighters of the People's Liberation Struggle in Macedonia against German Army and Bulgarian Axis-aligned forces which occupied Prilep early in the People's Liberation Struggle (WWII) during April of 1941. The Mogila Memorial complex in Prilep consists of memorial Urns and the common graves of fallen soldiers. Urns are constructed from marble, and reminiscent of the antique urns. Biggest urn in the Mogila complex has the symbol of the eternal flame at the top, which is symbol of Macedonian people's struggle for freedom. In the second part of the Mogila complex is the crypt which houses the remains of 462 fallen partisan fighters from Prilep and the neighboring places, whose names are inscribed on the marble slabs. The Mogila memorial monument continues to stand as a symbol of Prilep and is well maintained.

The tobacco seed spread along all continents since the 16th century taking the regions of warm climate, sun and diligent workers which would result in the best quality of aromatic plant "gold". This is the case with Prilep and the fertile Pelagonia field that write history closely connected with tobacco. The first tobacco Institute was the oldest scientific institution in the Balkans involved in genetic research and improvement of sort quality, production and models of production of tobacco and its products, established in Prilep i Macedonia and the Kingdom of Yugoslavia. The founder and long-term president of the Tobacco Institute was Rudolf Gornik, Yugoslav scientist for agriculture and founder of the tobacco science in Kingdom of Yugoslavia and Socialist Federative Republic of Yugoslavia. Rudolf Gornik completed in 1916 Gymnasium in Osijek and continued his education in Praha. It was his proposal to establish on 24 December 1924 the central experimental station for research of tobacco, the first and unique one in the Balkans. Thanks to professor Gornik and his assistants the Tobacco Institute in Prilep became the first scientific establishment in Kingdom of Yugoslavia and the Balkans to make genetic research and hybridisation on plants in creation of new and more resistant sorts of tobacco. In 1930 was created the first sort of the famous Prilep tobacco known today. In 1932 the Law on Tobacco was introduced which regulated that tobacco can be produced in the state only from tobacco seeds produced in the experimental station in Prilep. Professor Gornik became in 1939 the chief of the State monopoly for Tobacco in Belgrade. Foundations for the Tobacco Institute were laid down in November 1937, and construction was completed on 10 August 1939. The High school for Tobacco was founded in 1946 was where students from the whole socialist Yugoslavia learned on the Tobacco industry. Professor Gornik gave great contribution in modernization of tobacco production and research and creation of the new tobacco sorts suitable for the Pelagonia area. The new sorts of Tobacco were created Prilep 10-3/2, Prilep 12-2/1, Jaka Kire-ciler and Otlja, as well as new sorts of Virginia tobacco type. Rudolf Gornik was founder of the Tutun magazine in 1951, and later its editor in chief. Then Gornik left to Zagreb where he established the Tobacco Institute there. During his long career Gornik was greatly decorated and prized, and iin 1964 he became the honorary citizen of Prilep and the member of the Macedonian Academy of

Sciences. The Tobacco Museum was established in 1973 by dr Boško Babić 1973, as per memory of 100 years of organized production of tobacco in Prilep and 400 years of tobacco existence in the Ottoman Empire. The Prilep Tobacco Museum keeps and exhibits rich collection of some 4200 items for tobacco manufacture processing as well as some 750 wonderfully ornamented pipes and chibouks of *gold, silver, enamel, mother of pearl, ivory and bone of rhinoceros.* At the time of establishment of the Tobacco Museum they spent 13 German Marks of that time for collections and items.

The Church of SS Kiril and Metodius in Prilep was built between 1926 and 1936, close to the place of the former church from 1884. Bishop of Bitola Josip consecrated the foundations of the church, and Bishop Nikolaj Velimirovic consecrated the church when it was completed in 1936. The Orthodox church of SS Kiril and Metodius is impressive structure of the famous Belgrade architect Momir Korunovic, whose fruitful activities in the region, between the two world wars resulted in significant architectural accomplishments. The Church of SS Kiril and Metodius in Prilep was built in memory of King Petar Karadjordjevic and to commemorate the Serbian soldiers killed in this part of Macedonia in Prilep area and surroundings, during the First World War. The crypt of the SS Kiril and Metodius Church keeps remains of 1800 Serbina solders killed in the wars 1912-1918 in Prilep area."*Spiritual rule personified in non-canonic Macedonian Orthodox Church, consciously hide remaining bones of the Serbian soldiers martyres kept in the Memorial Church of SS Kiril and Metodius with ossuary in Prilep who gave their lives during the First Balkan War for liberation of Prilep and the area from the declining Ottoman Empire, and in 1918 their comrades-in-arms by breaking the Salonica Front have suppressed the new conquerers from Germany, Austria-Hungary and Bulgaria."* Miloš Meljanac

On 19 December 2008, the patron's day of Prilep, officially became part of the Guinness World Records. *80,191* cabbage rolls or 'sarma', were prepared for every citizen of town; thus Prilep attempted to set a Guinness World Record under the category of the largest cabbage dish. The traditional sarma was prepared by the skillful hands of 160 women volunteers of the Prerodba women association, NGO Mother-Tradition and the VMRO-DPMNE Union of women. The sarma in the size of a hazelnut, was prepared in the EURO Restaurant in Prilep, and within the course of 6 hours the 160 women prepared the 80,191 cabbage rolls ! In order to be authentic in taste and size, the sarmas were in miniature dimensions, 10×10 mm, and about a tonne of cabbage and 60 kilograms of rice was used. Each woman was set to prepare about 500 sarma rolls. It takes an enormous amount of skill to make them, since in a very small cabbage leaf one should wrap enough grains of rice to be boiled in the best way possible. The net weight of the Prilep sarma cabbage dish was exactly 544 kg. The previous record holder was the Serbian town of Novi Sad whose citizens prepared 6,400 sarma rolls, though Guinness notes that the Prilep volunteers intend to break a Guiness record and make up to 80,000 sarmas. For the celebration of Saint Nicholas, 19th December 2015, the town of Prilep offered and served 70.000 fast sarma rolls, along the blessing for well-being and happiness ! Those memorable skills and the unique well-preserved traditions are reconstructed and available to visitors in our famous Balkan Gastronomic tours !

Radika River

Radika River is the true pearl among the rivers of Macedonia, whose valley in West Macedonia is characterized a fragile ecosystem of unique ancient beech forests. Radika River features pure, clear and cool water of dark green color which is result of the calcium carbonate in it. Set between Mavrovo and Debar on one side, and on the Albanian side and Kichevo on the other side, the *Reka region* with the Radika River borders Shar Mountain on the northwest, Deshat Mountain on the south, the Korab and Krchin on the west and mountains of Bistra and Stogovo on the east.

Radika River rises on 2200 meters above sea level on the spectacular Bistra Mountain. From its source to the mouth of the river in Debar Lake, Radika River is 67 km long. The valley of Radika River is one of the most attractive and the most picturesque canyon-valleys in beautiful Macedonia. The Radika River canyon has been formed over millions of years breaking through the mountain sides of Bistra and Stogovo in the East and Korab and Deshat in the west. The canyon on the Radika River is truly enchanting with clear mountain water, surrounded by thick vegetation, as well as with the abundance of trout fish, which lures the fishing lovers. The scientists have researched over 30 caves, 10 meters long, in the upper course of the Radika River. Outstanding with its beauty is the 500 meters long "Simka" Cave.

The *Reka region* of Macedonia consists of several parts Gorna Reka, Golema Reka, Mijak region and Mala Reka region. Gorna Reka is the territory of the upper course of the Radika River with some mostly abandoned villages, as it used to be populated with Orthodox Serbs in the past, and nowadays with ethnic Albanians who spoke Albanian. The Dolna Reka region includes still active picturesque villages Zirovnica, Rostusha, Bitushe, Jance, Skudrinje... The region of Mala Reka covers the area along the flows of Mala, Tresonce and Gari rivers, as well as the part of the Stogovo Mountain, with following villages : Gari /wonderful tiny village on 1100 meters/, Tresonce, Lazaropole, Selce, Rosoki, Osoj and Mogorche. Population of the regions of Golema Reka and the Mala Reka consists of around 10000 Macedonian Mijaks who are either Orthodox or Muslim, and have always been advanced farmers or migrant workers. They have always been reputed fresco painters, wood carvers, brick-layers and mosaic artisans and nowadays they are some of the most sought after facade makers, tillers and bricklayers in Italy and Western Europe. Mijaks are also fantastic hosts in variety of local workshops with memorable culinary and lifestyle activities organized for our clients by our Macedonian partners !!!

Mijaci pl. Miyaks are the Serb tribe which settles the area of western part of the present North Macedonia in the course of the Radika River, the right tributary of Crni Drim River Black Drim River, that is known as the Reka region. Locals of the Reka region are known in other parts as Rekanci, but also Debarci for the fact that the nearest settlement is Debar, which they administratively belonged to during the Turkish reign. The term of Galičanci is also used, after the once largest Miyak village of Galicnik. The Serbian tribe of Mijaks Miyaks in present north-western Macedonia in the Mala Dolna Reka known as 'Mijacija' is the Serb ethnic group which belongs to the old Balkan population, that for long time resisted Bulgarization and communist movement of Macedonization. Mijaks are organized in tribal communities similar to tribes in Herzegovina, Littoral, Old Crna Gora Old Montenegro, Brda Hills, Metohija and Raska areas. Mijaks are also very similar to the Serbs on the other side of the Sar Mountain, in the Sirinic Zhupa of Metohija area, around Strpce and Brezovica settlements. The largest settlements populated by Mijaks are Lazaropolje, Galicnik, Gari, Bituse, Selce, Osoj and Susica. However, today among Mijaci-Mijaks only minority declares themselves as Serbs, while majority declares them the Macedonians, and those who would consider themselves as Bulgarians almost do not exist.

Saint Archangel Michael Monastery Štip

The hilltop stronghold, 150 meters high on the rocky hill over the town of Stip in east of Macedonia, with the monastery complex includes foundations of necropolis and settlements from the bronze and iron ages, thermal spas from the Roman period and numerous well preserved cultural-historical monuments from the middles ages. Stip was the largest cultural and trade center in eastern Macedonia since the ancient times. At the end of the rule of the Serbian king Stefan Decanski /Stephen of Decani Monastery/, and at the beginning of the reign of his son Dusan, there was the local lord Hrelja who governed the area of Stip. The governor Hrelja had built the Church dedicated to Saint Archangel Michael in the western part of hinterland of Stip, and gifted the shrine and the belonging estate to the Hilandar Monastery, which was later in 1332 confirmed by the tsar Dusan. The historian of that period testify : "This church of the ruler and military leader Hrelja still stands in Stip, on the Hisar hill, and is named the Fitija. Next to this church there are other churches of Old Serbia, beneath the Hisar hill the Church of Saint Prophet Elias the endowment of Konstantin Dejanovic from 1381, the Church of Saint Savior the endowment of duke Demetrios, erected in 1369, and the Church of Saint John the Baptist the endowment of ruler Jovan Probistipovic, built in 1350..."

The Church of Saint Archangel Michael is located under the Isar Fortress, built on the foundations of the antique Astibo and Byzantine Stypion, on a dominant hill between the Bregalnica and Otinja Rivers in East Macedonia. This shrine is the first one among the four Medieval churches erected beneath the fortification in a row making a cross. It is a small medieval church, built in the first half of the 14th century with a dome over the cross-shaped basis and with facades in layers of bricks and stone. During the restorations works, the paraklis dating from the 14th century was destroyed. The Church of Saint archangel Michael was erected by the Protosevastes Hrelya, the duke of Tsar Dušan, who is known in the Serbian epics as the „Relja krilatica" and who ruled the areas towards the border with Bulgaria and Byzantine Empire at that time. The church painting is preserved only in fragments which very poorly depict the images of Tzar Constantine and of his mother,

Holy Empress Helen, as well as the image of a holy warrior. The outside walls are beautifully decorated with blocks of processed stone and the only entrance is on the west side. There is a bell tower next to the church. The Church of the Saint Savior in Stip is set on the left shore of the Otinja River, on the road leading to the Novo selo village. The Saint Savior church is located on the flat rock and attracts attention of the visitors' eyes by its tiny dimensions and the cozy and secluded appearance with the surrounding necropolis and numerous tombs.

Holy Archangel Michael Monastery Varos

Holy Archangel Michael Monastery Varos is one of the most beautiful and the most significant Medieval Monastery in Macedonia, located within the picturesque landscape of impressive granite rocks Varosh area, near the town of Prilep. The Towers of Marko /Markovi kuli town of Marko/ was settlement built on the massive stone outcropping containing a stronghold first built in the 2nd or 3rd century BC. The Medieval town of Prilep was at the foothill of the rocky Varosh area, known as the Markovi kuli the towers of Marko, built on the place of the Roman settlement of *Ceramiae.* The Varosh complex resembles the 'eagle's nest' among the magnificent rocks, on the south-western side of the Markovi kuli the Marko's towers. The Varosh Monastery complex in Prilep includes foundations of necropolis and settlements from the Bronze and Iron ages, thermal spas from the Roman period and numerous well preserved cultural-historical monuments from the Middles ages. Varosh area dates from the ancient history, built for defensive purposes, but it persisted through the Medieval period. The remains of preserved Medieval Varosh churches undoubtedly prove the intense life that evolved in the Middle Ages. In the 14th century the King Marko Mrnjavcevic built upon this a defensive stronghold. After death of King Marko, in the Maritza Battle in 1395, the town of Prilep was conquered by the Turks, who built the town we see today, whose remains are pretty well preserved.

The Holy Archangel Michael Monastery complex in Varosh includes the wonderful church dedicated to Saint archangel Michael, dating probably either from the 10th century or from the second half of the 12th century. The Varosh complex also contains the beautiful Dormitory facing the broad valley below, built in the 19th century by the Prilep guilds which features wonderful characteristics of the town architecture and guild inscriptions in the dormitory rooms.

The church of the Holy archangel Michael in Varos is one nave structure, with the dome above the central part, and a semi-circular apse on the eastern side. The beautiful church was originally constructed of layers of bricks and stone, and dominates the Varos area. The Saint Archangel's church Varos features an open porch with a bell on the west side. There is only one window preserved until today, on the original upper part of the southern facade of the western part of the Holy Archangel Michael church.

Legend has it that King Marko built the church with stolen funds, resulting in a curse on the church and its eventual abandonment. The legend continues that the Archangel Michael spoke to a woman named Mary in a dream and based on this dream, Mary was able to rebuild the monastery with help from people in the Prilep area. In folk tradition, are mentioned the chapel dedicated to Saint Luke, while in the charter of King Dusan, along with the Treskavec Monastery are also listed several churches : *St. John the Baptist, St. George, Sveti Vrachi /Holy Healers/, St. Theodore and St. Demetrius. From the number of churches built in the Varosh area, today are preserved: Saint Nicholas /Sveti Nikola, built in 1299/, Monastery of St. Archangel Michael /Manastir Sveti Arhangel Mihajlo/, St. Demetrius /Sveti Dimitrije/, St. Athanasius /Sveti Atanasije/, Saints*

Peter and Paul /Sveti Petar i Pavle/ and chuch of the Holy Virgin /Sveta Bogorodica/.

Visitors can reach the Holy Archangel's Monastery in Varos by foot, using the walk stone trail which connects the monasteries in this area or by car using the asphalt road.

From the remains of the Markovi kuli town of Marko spreads magic panorama of Prilep and the Pelagonia Plain, with magnificent mountains in the hinterland.

Saint George Monastery Kurbinovo village

The church dedicated to Saint George is situated in the Prespa Lake area, near the tiny picturesque village of Kurbinovo, embraced by the Pelister Mountain-National Park. According to the time of its fresco-decoration as per the Greek inscription in the northern side, it is assumed that the Church of Saint George Monastery in Kurbinovo village has been built in 1191. The inscription in Kurbinovo church was completed in black letters, in four lines, on bright, redish-brownish background, on the spot of trapezoid shape, in the eastern side of the constructed altar table. That was the time when Byzantine Empire ruled territory of present Republic of Macedonia, the time after the reign of Tzar Samuil, the first Slavo-Macedonian Emperor, and the founder of the first medieval Slavo-Macedonian state. However there are still no reliable documented data on time of construction and the donor of Saint George Church in Kurbinovo village. The Church of Saint George in Kurbinovo village was built by stone, while bricks were used for construction of the altar double lancet window, arch-vaults and lunettes above the entrance, and partially around them. The Kurbinovo church was plastered in the outside, with fresco technique used to imitate the construction with stone and bricks, before the church had been fresco painted inside and on the western facade. In the 19th century, the Kurbinovo Church was renovated, and in the first decades of the 20th century a wooden ceiling and the porch were built, and the southern and the northern entrances were closed and transformed into two windows.

What impresses and amazes in this church is its fresco-painting, which, coupled by the one in the church of Sveti Panteleimon Monastery near Skopje, represents an original and a peak of the artistic mastery in the times of the art of Comnenes in Macedonia. On the west facade of the Saint George Monastery in Kurbinovo, there are visible remnants of frescoes with depictions of female and male characters in full size, vested in imperial clothes, as well as a figure of a church nobleman. It is most probably a depiction of the people who built the original small church of Saint George.

The fresco-painting in the interior of the church of Saint George in Kurbinovo village is divided into three zones. The drawing is expressive, dynamic, with accentuated slenderness, vivaciousness and movement of the painted figures, with the dominant feeling of the inner experience of the characters in the dramatic scenes. Typical is the depiction of the drapes that are vivacious in baroque style, with a great number of animated folds. The frescoes of Saint George Church in Kurbinovo village illustrate scenes from the life of Jesus Christ and Virgin Mary. In the altar apse of Saint George Church in Kurbinovo village, the composition Annunciation is painted, that has made this church exclusive and a part of the annals of the peak achievements of the Byzantine fresco-painting. The depiction of the Archangel Gabriel stands out and it has almost become a symbol and landmark of the church in Kurbinovo. Part of the Saint Gabriel fresco of Saint George in Kurbinovo village is depicted on the Macedonian banknote of 50 denars. Interesting and rare are the depictions of Jesus Christ and the patron of the church, Saint George, from the north and the south wall, with a monumental size. Outstanding among the frescoes of Church of

Saint George in Kurbinovo village are the portraits of Ana and its daughter Mary, the Mother of God, painted in the lower zone of the south wall of the naos, as well as the portraits of the Macedonian en-lighteners Cyril and Methodius, in the altar space. The depiction of St. Methodius is its oldest portrait known in the entire Slavic-Byzantine world. Opposite from them, there is the figure of St. Clement of Ohrid. The fresco-painting of Saint George Monastery in Kurbinovo village is a synthesis of in-fusible into a single entity, a junction of its pinnacle elegance and the high expressiveness.

Saint Joachim Monastery Osogovo

The gorgeous Osogovo Mountains are located in the northeastern Macedonia, between the cities of Kriva Palanka in the north, Delchevo and Kochani in the south, Probishtip and Kratovo in the west, and its eastern parts are set in the territory of Bulgaria. *Osogovo Mountains* highest point is the peak of *Ruen* (2252 meters), at the very border between Macedonia and Bulgaria. The Monastery of Saint Joachim of Osogovo is considered as one of the most beautiful monasteries in Macedonia and is hidden in tranquility and lush forests and greenery of Osogovo Mountains peaks, at the altitude of 825 meters, in the village of Babin Zub, approachable by the winding road.

The anchorite Joachim lived secluded life and performed various miracles in the place called Sarandopor, which means the forty dales, in the remote Osogovo Mountains cave, like famous anchorites saints of *John of Rila, Prohorus of Pčinja and Gabriel of Lesnovo did*. Sometimes around 1105 anchorite Joachim died in his hermitage. Saint Joachim of Osogovo Monastery is also known as the Sarandopor Monastery. During the reign of the Byzantine Tsar Manojlo Comnenus the cult of the Saint Joachim was very strong, when monk Teodor had built a tiny church dedicated to the Birth of the Holy Virgin where he brought the relics of the Saint. The church of Saint Joachim of Osogovo is cross-shaped, with calottes and the eight-sided dome, sitting on the junction of crosses. Only ornamental fragments on the northern side of the altar remained from the oldest layer of frescoes.

Monastery of Saint Joachim of Osogovo is first mentioned during the reign of the Bulgarian Tsar Kaloyan /1196 1207/. In the year of 1330 it was restored by the Serbian King Stefan Dečanski /Stefan of Dečani Monastery/ who stayed here before the famous Battle of Velbužd /present day Kyustendil/. The Turkish sultan Mehmed II also stayed in the Osogovo Monastery before his military invasions into Bosnia. Devastating earthquake in 1585 significantly destroyed the Osogovo monastic structures that were rebuilt by the donation from Russia. Around 1762 the Monastery of Saint Joachim of Osogovo experienced hard times when part of the holy relics disappeared. Turks banned restoration and free celebration of the Christian feasts.

The large church dedicated to Saint Joachim of Osogovo is monumental stone three-nave structure with 12 cupolas, 7 small and 5 big cupolas, which was built by masters of Andrej Damjanov Zografski with the donation of Stefan Mladenov from Kriva Palanka. Holy relics of Saint Joachim of Osogovo are located to the right of the church entry. There are some gravestones next to the church. The most impressive wall paintings of Saint Joachim of Osogovo Monastery were executed by Dimitar Andonov Papradishki and date from the recent period 1932 and 1933. One of the most characteristic frescoes is "the sermon of Saint Paul", where the hand of the artist carried in it profane elements. On this remarkable fresco of Saint Joachim of Osogovo Monastery the national costume of Kriva Palanka is shining with all its beauty and rusticity. Other frescoes of the Osogovo Monastery depict the Serbian kings, rulers and saints: on the south wall there are portraits of *Saint Tsar Uros,*

Saint Tsar Lazar, Saint King Milutin, Saint Stefan Decanski, and on the northern wall there are depicted Saint Nikodim /Serbian archbishop/ and Saint Stefan Prvovencani /the First-crowned/. Iconostasis of Saint Joachim of Osogovo Monastery contains two valuable icons, probably painted by Hristo Dimitrov of the Samokovo school of painters. The spring believed by faithful to have medicinal features is situated next to the church.

The Monastery of Saint Joachim of Osogovo encompasses several centrally heated dormitories for accommodation of visitors, with the total capacity of 120 beds, including 6 apartments, that provide pleasant stay throughout the year, and in winter as well. There is the restaurant with 40 seats which offers choice of tasty food and good quality of service. The meeting hall with 80 seats is the part of the Osogovo monastic complex. located in the natural and spiritual ambiance and provides good conditions for various events and meetings which do not disturb the overall spirituality of this place of worship.

Saint George Monastery Staro Nagoričane village

The Monastery of Saint George is located near to the village of Staro Nagoricane in the north-eastern part of Macedonia, 13 km east from Kumanovo, on the slopes of Kozjak Mountain and in the vast and picturesque Pcinja River valley. The tiny village of Staro Nagoricane at present has 556 inhabitants of whom 452 declared themselves as the Serb nationality in the last census.

The original Church of Saint George Monastery was built in 1071 by the Byzantine Emperor Roman IV Diogenes. As one of his many endowments, Serbian King Milutin restored thoroughtly the Nagoricane church in 1313 after the great victory against the Ottoman Turks. The church of Saint George Monastery in Staro Nagoricane features the base of elongated inscribed cross given that the original sacral building was basilica with five domes. The basis of the earlier Nagoricane church erected of stone, was leveled to the half of the present day height during the reconstruction and on the very basis the new church of bricks and stones was constructed that can be seen on the altar apse which was originally of the semi-circular shape covered with the new five-sides dome. According to some researches, the church of Saint George Monastery in Staro Nagoricane village was constructed by the same masters of King Milutin who built the Holy Virgin of Ljevis Church on the preserved basis. The special feature of the church in Staro Nagoricane are the main icons that were done in specific *al fresco* technique directly on the mortar which make this church the unique one among the Serbian shrines. The church of Saint George Monastery in Staro Nagoricane village is covered by the stone blocks and is very well preserved until the present time. The original frescoes of Nagoricane church are considered the most beautiful in so-called "Vardar style". Bulgarian emperor Mihajlo III Šišman (1322-1330), killed in the Battle of Velbuzhd is buried in the church.

In the time of the Serbian rule, the Saint George Monastery of Staro Nagoricane was in ruins and the monastery was deserted. The ground floor of the church was preserved and used in the reconstruction works of the new shrine, so the preserved part influenced the final form of the building. Frescoes of Saint George Monastery as well as in the major endowments of King Milutin were painted by fresco painters Michael and Eutychius. It is believed that those frescoes have large similarities with decoration of Gracanica Monastery and the Church of the Holy Virgin of Ljevis. On the shield of one of the saint warriors it is written : ….."by the hand of the Michael the fresco-painter…". The same thing was done by the second painter Eutychius on the shield of the Saint Theodore Theron. When painters have completed the works here : …."they could have been satisfied as they have completed their greatest and the most important work"...

The scenes of the calendar /minologue/ is similar to those in the Monastery of Gracanica, painted just after the Nagoricino church, as the King's Milutin last endowment. King Milutin is depicted holding the church model, which is very truly presented figure. Besides the fact that every shrine built or reconstructed by King Milutin who was obviously great donor of the shrines at his time with architectural and painting similarities, depictions of the ruler King Milutin are always different. In Gracanica Monastery angels blessed by Christ bring the crown to the King Milutin, while in Nagoricino church, the patron of the shrine, Saint George, handles the sward to the King as the gift to the endowment. In regard with the pose and attire of the King Milutin, they are similar to those in Studenica and Gracanica Monasteries. The depiction of the donor in Nagoricino features the gesture of the patron of the shrine, Saint George, to whom the king gifts the church. Saint George is turned towards the King Milutin with raised right hand while in the left hand he handles the sward to be given to the King. This scene is connected with the victory against the Turkish army from the year of the construction of the church, which is evidenced by the inscription of the building. No matter either the church was erected as the fulfillment of the promises before the battle of it was the gratitude of the victory, King Milutin is depicted in triumph. There is no usual scene of the donor with the model of the church lead by the Holy Virgin or the patron of the shrine. Here are scenes of saint warriors that were executed for the Christianity.

The Saint Emperor Constantine and his mother Helena are depicted besides the royal couple within the endowers' composition. King Milutin is compared in the literate resources with Emperor Constantine or he is considered as his disciple ...."similar to the famous Constantine"..... "dependable to the God's help and worshiping and rising of his heritage"…. The patron of the church, Saint George is depicted several times. Since the scenes depictions in the Monastery of Saint George in Staro Nagoričino is the most comprehensive Medieval complex, its depictions can be regarded as the foundations of the many more famous scenes. Numerous details from the late-Byzantine scenes are first mentioned in the scenes in Nagoricino, dependable from the "Erminije". One of those scenes has significance and the feature of the fresco-icon which stands where usually priest sits, which confirm the presence of the Priest Venjamin who was in charge of the fulfillment of the King's intents on construction and fresco decoration.

The monastery church is decorated with colorful bricks from the outside. Two tripartite windows on the southern and the northern peaks of the inscribed cross are specially rich in decoration as well as byfora on the narthex above the entrance which makes column rolled-up. Above the entrance door there is large stone inscription of King Milutin and King's monograms decorate capitols of two columns located on the western entrance to the church. The iconostasis of St George's Monastery in Staro Nagoricane village has been made of stone and consists of four columns with capitols and architrave.

" The Zabel Monastery above the Staro Nagoricano village in South Serbia was the center of the Kumanovo Uprising in 1878 where the Serbian rebells and reputed local Serbs gave oath for liberation and union with the Princedom of Serbia. Bulgarian occupiers looted and demolished the Zabel Monastery in 1915. Tradition has it that this monastery was erected by Prince Lazar. The Church of the Most Holy Virgin of the Zabel Monastery was constructed in 1330.

In 1900 the reputed local of Kumanovo, Filip Dimkovic joined the monastic family. Previously his family declined when his third wife died, and soon the only child, so he remained alone in the house. In his great greef he completely turned to God and the church, and donated his whole wealth of 4000 dinars to the Zabel Monastery. In the monastery he received management of the whole monastic estate….. In 1924 there in the monastery lived Russian monks refugees who took care about the shrine. Negligence and abandonment in the 20th century led to the complete damage of the Zabel Monastery dormitory, stables and economic structures. Through centuries the Church of the Ascension of the Most Holy Virgin remained in good condition, with pretty well preserved values and beuties created by its constructors. Yet, few years ago, vandals looted four icons which were more than 150 years old. Icon of the Holy Virgin was literary crashed out from the altar space. Author of stolen icons was the famous icon painter Dičo Zograf. Scholar claim that the value of stolen reliquaries is simply priceless. The older locals of this area say that this was the first theft of icones, but also that the destiny of this church is very sad". Hadži Miloš Marinković Srpstvo u Makedoniji

Saint Joachim Monastery Osogovo

The gorgeous Osogovo Mountains are located in the northeastern Macedonia, between the cities of Kriva Palanka in the north, Delchevo and Kochani in the south, Probishtip and Kratovo in the west, and its eastern parts are set in the territory of Bulgaria. *Osogovo Mountains* highest point is the peak of *Ruen* (2252 meters), at the very border between Macedonia and Bulgaria. The Monastery of Saint Joachim of Osogovo is considered as one of the most beautiful monasteries in Macedonia and is hidden in tranquility and lush forests and greenery of Osogovo Mountains peaks, at the altitude of 825 meters, in the village of Babin Zub, approachable by the winding road.

The anchorite Joachim lived secluded life and performed various miracles in the place called Sarandopor, which means the forty dales, in the remote Osogovo Mountains cave, like famous anchorites saints of *John of Rila, Prohorus of Pčinja and Gabriel of Lesnovo did*. Sometimes around 1105 anchorite Joachim died in his hermitage. Saint Joachim of Osogovo Monastery is also known as the Sarandopor Monastery. During the reign of the Byzantine Tsar Manojlo Comnenus the cult of the Saint Joachim was very strong, when monk Teodor had built a tiny church dedicated to the Birth of the Holy Virgin where he brought the relics of the Saint. The church of Saint Joachim of Osogovo is cross-shaped, with calottes and the eight-sided dome, sitting on the junction of crosses. Only ornamental fragments on the northern side of the altar remained from the oldest layer of frescoes.

Monastery of Saint Joachim of Osogovo is first mentioned during the reign of the Bulgarian Tsar Kaloyan /1196 1207/. In the year of 1330 it was restored by the Serbian King Stefan Dečanski /Stefan of Dečani Monastery/ who stayed here before the famous Battle of Velbužd /present day Kyustendil/. The Turkish sultan Mehmed II also stayed in the Osogovo Monastery before his military invasions into Bosnia. Devastating earthquake in 1585 significantly destroyed the Osogovo monastic structures that were rebuilt by the donation from Russia. Around 1762 the Monastery of Saint Joachim of Osogovo experienced hard times when part of the holy relics disappeared. Turks banned restoration and free celebration of the Christian feasts.

The large church dedicated to Saint Joachim of Osogovo is monumental stone three-nave structure with 12 cupolas, 7 small and 5 big cupolas, which was built by masters of Andrej Damjanov Zografski with the donation of Stefan Mladenov from Kriva Palanka. Holy relics of Saint Joachim of Osogovo are located to the right of the church entry. There are some gravestones next to the church.

The most impressive wall paintings of Saint Joachim of Osogovo Monastery were executed by Dimitar Andonov Papradishki and date from the recent period 1932 and 1933. One of the most characteristic frescoes is "the sermon of Saint Paul", where the hand of the artist carried in it profane elements. On this remarkable fresco of Saint Joachim of Osogovo Monastery the national costume of Kriva Palanka is shining with all its beauty and rusticity. Other frescoes of the Osogovo Monastery depict the Serbian kings, rulers and saints: on the south wall there are portraits of *Saint Tsar Uros, Saint Tsar Lazar, Saint King Milutin, Saint Stefan Decanski, and on the northern wall there are depicted Saint Nikodim /Serbian archbishop/ and Saint Stefan Prvovencani /the First-crowned/.* Iconostasis of Saint Joachim of Osogovo Monastery contains two valuable icons, probably painted by Hristo Dimitrov of the Samokovo school of painters. The spring believed by faithful to have medicinal features is situated next to the church.

The Monastery of Saint Joachim of Osogovo encompasses several centrally heated dormitories for accommodation of visitors, with the total capacity of 120 beds, including 6 apartments, that provide pleasant stay throughout the year, and in winter as well. There is the restaurant with 40 seats which offers choice of tasty food and good quality of service. The meeting hall with 80 seats is the part of the Osogovo monastic complex. located in the natural and spiritual ambiance and provides good conditions for various events and meetings which do not disturb the overall spirituality of this place of worship.

Saint John Bigorski Monastery

Sveti Jovan Bigorski Monastery Saint John Bigorski Monastery is Orthodox Monastery located in west Macedonia, on the road connecting Gostivar and Debar, in the vicinity of the tiny Rostuse village, in wonderful eco environment. Sveti Jovan Bigorski Monastery Saint John the Baptist Bigorski Monastery is the 19th century monastery standing on the foundations of the earlier shrine, on the slopes of the picturesque Bistra Mountain, within the area of the *Mavrovo National Park*, above the banks of the gorgeous Radika River. This is the area of Stara Srbija Old Serbia widely renowed for extraordinary skilled local woodcarvers who accomplished marvelous wood-carved iconostasis in the Balkans. The present Monastery of Sveti Jovan Bigorski Saint John Bigorski was constructed in the unique *Miyak-Debar style of architecture* over the remains of an older church dating from 1021, which by some historical records was the endowment of the *Serbian King Holy Jovan Vladimir Sveti Jovan Vladimir. Slatina is one of the important settlements in the Srednja Debarca area at the foot of the Ilinske planine mountains. It is believed that once at the site of Bigor there was the Sveti Jovan Bigorski Monastery, which was in inexplicable way transferred to the present location in the Radika River Valley.*

At the entrance to the church of the Sveti Jovan Bigorski Monastery is outer narthex with marble partition a tryphora which closes approach to the central part and fulfills the space with unusual quietness and semi-darkness. Interior and outer narthex of the Saint John Bigorski church are fresco painted by local fresco painters from the nearby Lazaropole village with scenes of the Christ life and passions while in the outer narthex is painted row of the Serbian Medieval kings until the Kosovo Battle in 1389. In the dome of the large cupola is depicted Christ Pantocrator who blesses with his right hand the faithful and holds a Gospel in his left hand. In the 16th century during the reign of the notorious Sultan Selim I 1512/1520 Turks destroyed to the ground the Sveti Jovan Bigorski Saint John Bigorski Monastery when only a small church remained, that had been quickly restored afterwards. The Saint Jovan Bigorski

Monastery Sveti Jovan Bigorski was restored in 1743 by the monk Ilarion and local Mijaks, when several monastic cells were added. At the beginning of the 19th century, during the management of Abbot Arsenius, the Monastery of Saint John Bigorski Sveti Jovan Bigorski was expanded and enjoyed support of numerous Serbs of the Mala Reka area Mijak benefactors, being the center of spiritual life of the local Mijaks /Miyaks/.

The ornamented wonderfully wood-carved iconostasis of the Bigorski Monastery church was elaborated in the 1830s which belongs to the most fascinating work of this monastery. The iconostasis of Saint John Bigorski Monastery is divided into six horizontal bands. The first zone is basically composed of rectangular fields that feature ornaments of flora and fauna. The second zone, which moved throne icons ends with a figure of an eagle with spread wings. The third area of the iconostasis is divided into three smaller horizontal parts that are symmetrically distributed angels, grapes and vines, etc. Above them are two rows of icons with depictions of apostles. In the center of the Bigorski Monastery iconostasis is the large cross with the Christ Crucifixion. Besides the iconostasis of the Sveti Jovan Bigorski Monastery, the arch priest's throne and the prior's chair had been manufactured by the wood-carvers group of Petre Fylipovic-Garkata from the Gari village, with the help of his brother Marko and with active participation of a number of distinguished Miyak wood-carvers. The zographs Michail and his son Dimitar from Samarina, Epirus village, at that time painted the throne icons, the festive icons and the icons of the holy apostles for the iconostasis in the Bigorski monastery. With the accomplishment of the Bigorski iconostasis, *Miyak wood carvers have acquired a reputation of the best and the most wanted wood carvers on the entire Balkan Peninsula.* Many scenes, compositions and individual figures have been engraved in the iconostasis, being presented in movement and with an expressed dramatics in some scenes, like the scene with Beheading of Saint John. The beauty of the Bigorski Monastery iconostasis is enriched with many animals and birds, interwoven with floral ornaments with a realistic presentment of a grape vine, flowers of narcissus, garden roses, oriental fruits, as well as the favorite motif of the Miyak wood carvers, cracked pomegranates. It may be rightfully stated that the creations of the Mijak wood carvers on the iconostasis of the Bigorski monastery are in-suppressed either by the ones on the Holy Mountain or the works of the Epirus wood carvers, not to mention the Samokov and Treven wood carvers.

Mijaci pl. Miyaks are the Serb tribe which settles the area of western part of the present North Macedonia in the course of the Radika River, the right tributary of Crni Drim River Black Drim River, that is known as the Reka region. Locals of the Reka region are known in other parts as Rekanci, but also Debarci for the fact that the nearest settlement is Debar, which they administratively belonged to during the Turkish reign. The term of Galičanci is also used, after the once largest Miyak village of Galicnik. The area of Mala Reka in West Macedonia is covered with typical and pure settlements of Miyaks, that are for long time famous in the art history as sources of construction, painters and woodcarvers : Galičnik, Sušica, Tresonče, Lazaropole, Gari, Osoj. Kopaničarstvo woodcarving of Miyaks is one of the most significant phenomenon of traditional heritage and art of the South Slavs. Works of the Miyak woodcarvers feature prominent floral ornamentation in which human figures were woven with great artistic skills into figurative compositions of Biblical scenes. The Serbian tribe of Mijaks Miyaks in present north-western Macedonia in the Dolna Reka known as Mijacija is the Serb ethnic group that for long time resisted Bulgarization and communist movement of Macedonization. Mijaks are organized in tribal communities similar to the original Serbian tribes in Herzegovina, Littoral, Old Crna Gora Old Montenegro, Brda Hills, Metohija and

Raska areas. Mijaks are also very similar to the Serbs on the other side of the Sar Mountain, in the Sirinic Zhupa of Metohija area, around Strpce and Brezovica settlements. The largest settlements populated by Mijaks are Lazaropolje, Gari, Bituse, Selce, Osoj and Susica. However, today among Mijaks only minority declares themselves as Serbs, while majority declares them the Macedonians, and those who would consider themselves as Bulgarians almost do not exist.

Built on a steep mountain slope surrounded by dense woods and rocky hills of serene West Macedonia, the Sveti Jovan Bigorski Monastery is reminiscent of the cliff top monasteries of Mount Athos in Greece. As this monastery is dedicated to Saint John the Baptist, the faithful believe that icons with his image are blessed with a miraculous healing power. The monastery of Sveti Jovan Bigorski also houses a small silver coffin containing alleged relics of Saint John and remarkable collection of handwritten manuscripts. On the outer walls of the Sveti Jovan Bigorski Monastery are frescoes painted by the famous Miyak fresco-painters from Lazaropole village, which depict only the *Serbian rulers and kings of the Nemanic Dynasty until the Kosovo Battle*. The Sveti Jovan Bigorski Monastery complex includes a dining room and old monastic dormitory, a tower, a charnel house and two fountains spilling over with fresh water.

Saint John Bigorski Monastery Sveti Jovan Bigorski is one of the most beautiful monasteries in the Balkans and comprises the unique altar masterly wood-carved in deep carves. The chief master was Petar Filipov from then village of Gari, a representative of the Debar woodcarving school, who, in cooperation with his brother Marko and several other assistants, worked for six years on this masterpiece. The icons in the iconostasis of Sveti Jovan Bigorski Monastery were painted by icon- painter Michail and his son Dimitar. Besides the iconostasis, the wood-carvers also elaborated the prelate's throne and the abbot's chair in the church, whose northers features marvelous mural paintings of St. Clement of Ohrid, St. Naum, St. George and other Orthodox saints. The Serbian tribe of Miyaks in the present northwestern Macedonia are the Serb ethnic group that for long time had resisted the Bulgarization and the Communist Macedonization. The Miyaks are organized by the tribal system and clans, likewise the tribes in Herzegovina, the Littoral, Old Crna Gora, the Brda Hills, Metohija and Raska. The Miyaks have many similarities with the Serbs living on the other side of the Sar Planina Mountain, in the Sirinicka zupa of Metohija, in Strpce and Brezovica settlements. The largest Miyak settlements and villages are Lazaropolje, Galicnik, Gari, Bituše, Selce, Osoj and Sušica. Nowadays among the Mijaks-Miyak population only a small minority declares themselves as the Serbs, as the majority are Macedonians, while those who declare themselves as the Bulgarians almost do not exist. Every Miyak family greatly respects and maintains the unique custom of celebration of the Patron Saint *Krsna slava or the Sluzba*, while the center of spiritual life is the Monastery of Saint Jovan Bigorski. Miyaks had preserved their unique customs and dialect that origin from the Nemanjic Dynasty realm.

Saint John Bigorski Sveti Jovan Bigorski Monastery is the shrine frequented by numerous visitors to Macedonia and the Balkans from all over the world.

Saint Nicholas Monastery Psaca

Saint Nicholas Monastery in Psaca village is located 14 km away from Kriva Palanka in eastern Macedonia. The Medieval Psaca Monastery is set in the northern part of the western foothill of the Osogovo Mountains, in the beautiful forests by the village of same name with population of 538 Macedonians according to the 2002 census. The Saint Nicholas Monastery in Psaca village has been built as the joint endowment of the Serb noble family of Paskachic, the sebastocrator Vlatko and his father Paskach, whose name might influenced the name of the village. The Paskach family was prominent Serb landlords who ruled the Slavishte area during the reign of Tsar Dusan and his son Uros. The Paskach family was in close relationship with the noble Mrnjavcevic family. There are not many historical records on the Vlatko's life, it is assumed that he got killed in the Maritza Battle in 1371, and left his juvenile son Ugljesa. Ugljesa was close associate of despot Stefan Lazarevic and ruler of the area of Vranje, Inogost and Presevo, but his possessions were later taken by the Dejanovic Family members.

Although there are insufficient and rare historical evidences on the construction of the Psaca Monastery, it is assumed that the construction of the tiny monastery church had been completed around 1354. The original church of the Psaca Monastery used to have the base in the form of elongated inscribed cross with a single dome above the central part, and the narthex which also had a dome and the stone roof. The dome was later removed, so that the present form of the Monastery church of Saint Nicholas reminds on the three-nave basilica, rather than the form of elongated cross church.

The original architectural appearance of the Psaca Monastery church has been preserved up to the present day, while the inscriptions around the picturesque portraits, painted between 1365 til 1371, which feature fine details of lively compositions, have been partially destroyed by Bulgarian schovinists, during the enemy occupation between 1916 and 1918, due to their intention to erase every clue of the Serbian origins. Portraits which adorn the walls of the Church of Saint Nicholas in Psaca are significant not only for their historical, but also for the ethnographic aspects. On the northern wall are depicted portraits of Tsar Uros (1355-1371) and

King Vukašin Mrnjavčević who were simultaneously rulers on the throne for some period of history (co-ruler king 1365-1369, independent ruler 1369-1371). Realistic depiction where the co-ruler King Vukašin stays right from Tsar Uros, clearly testifies on ruling hierarchy in the Serbian Medieval Kingdom. On the southern wall of the Saint Nicholas church in Psaca village are painted true depictions of the donor and his family Prince Paskač holding a church in his hands, together with his son Vlatko as the co-endower, Paskac's wife princess Ozra, Vladislava wife of Vlatko, and their three sons Stefan, Uroš and Uglješa.

There is little historical evidence about the Serbian nobleman Vlatko who dedicated this church to the Chilandari Monastery in 1358. However, the founding charter which attributes the Psaca Church to the Holy Virgin of the Chilandari Monastery, issued by the nobleman Vlatko is kept at the Chilandari Monastery. Significance of frescoes of the Saint Nicholas Monastery in Psaca is attested by historical data on its founders and their families. Nobleman Vlatko is here attributed sebastocrator which is the status entitled to the closes relatives to the rulers. The Charter from 1358 confirms that aristocrat Vlatko at the time of its issue was still considered the nobleman, which means that he got the sebastocrator status by his marriage with the girl from the ruler s house. His wire Vladislava most probably origins from the family of King Vukašin, who was at that time the co-ruler on the Serbian throne together with Tsar Uroš. As in the Middle Ages it was customs to name heirs with names of their ancestors, we may assume that Vladislava comes from the house of Despot Uglješa, brother of King Vukašin. That is how Vlatko, brother-in-law of the king got status of sebastocrator. Unfortunately there are not historical traces on the other member of the family, except for the youngest son Uglješa, who was mentioned during the reign of Despot Stefan Lazarevic in 1402 after glorious return from the Battle of Angora, then in 1410 on boats who carried Despot Stefan to the Prince Mirce of Wallachia and in 1412 during the campaign of ruler Musa to the Novo Brdo fortress. Later he got the title of kesar /ceasar/the ruler of the particular area, when he become known as the ruler of the Vranje, Inogost and Presevo towns. One of his sons is buried in the Ljubostinja Monastery, in Central Serbia, where on the grave stone it is inscribed : 'Stefan, son of the ćesar Uglješa'.

Portraits of the Church of Saint Nicholas Monastery in Psača belong to the most beautiful and best accomplished among the Serbian Medieval paintings of Macedonia. Along to the fact that the well-preserved frescoes of the Psaca Monastery truly depict members of the old Serbian noble family, they also provide important evidences for studying the lavish royal costumes of the Medieval Serbia. Besides the realistic depictions of historical personalities, frescoes of the Psaca Monastery also emanate scenes from live of Saint Nicholas, and compositions of the Ascension of the Holy Virgin and Communion of Apostles. Some additional frescoes were painted in the 19th century and in the beginning of the 20th century by the fresco painter Dimitrie Andonov Papradiski who used his recognizable talent to depict characters of several saints on the west facade of the church. The outer facade and walls of the Saint Nicholas Monastery in Psaca are richly decorated with stone ornaments and sculpture. On the western entrance to the church there was an inscription destroyed in 1876 as it mentioned Tsar Uroš and King Vukašin.

Saint Panteleimon Monastery Nerezi village

The Monastery of Saint Panteleimon in the village of Nerezi is the old, wonderfully preserved Byzantine Church from the middle of the 12th century that is situated in the village of Gornji Nerezi close to Skopje, on the wonderful Vodno Mountain. The Monastery of

Sveti Panteleimon, situated 6 km from the center of Skopje, on the slopes of Vodno Mountain, is an essential visit for anyone interested in the Byzantine art. The frescoes in St Panteleimon brought big changes in the development of the Byzantine art and Macedonian in particular and gave basis to suppose that local painters, though reared in the tradition of decorative Byzantine painting, could make brave steps even in the 12th and the 13th centuries towards a new art which was later, in the 14th and the 15th centuries in Italy known as the Renaissance Art.

The church and monastery are both dedicated to Saint Panteleimon, the patron of physicians. According to the Greek inscription on the marble plaque above the entrance to the nave, it is clear that the Saint Panteleimon Church has been built in 1164 by Alexius Angelus Comnenus, the relative of the Byzantine Tzar Manojlo I Comnenus. The Monastery of St Panteleimon was first mentioned in 1300 in the founding Charter of Serbian King Milutin /1282 -1321/ in which it was attested as the metochion of the Saint George Monastery in Staro Nagoricane village. The Church of Saint Panteleimon Monastery has base of the cross inscribed in rectangle with four small domes over the angles of the church and a large dome above the central part of the church with narthex, what makes it similar to the Church of Saint George in Staro Nagoricano and Matejce Monastery. The Saint Panteleimon Church has been built by group of talented unknown master-builders of ordinary blocks of stone and bricks with great artistry that merged into multicolored surfaces. Narthex with the semi-circular vault was added on the western side of the church.

The Saint Panteleimon Monastery in Gorno Nerezi village is known for its outstanding frescoes, exceptional in their style and aesthetics. Frescoes of the Saint Panteleimon Monastery have been painted by anonymous masters of the rank of the *best Byzantine imperial frescoes painters of the 12th century* and represent the most significant depictions of the Byzantine paintings and the best depictions of the Byzantine arts of the Comnenos era. The fresco paintings in the narthex of the St. Panteleimon church in Nerezi are only partly preserved, and by their thematic character, they can be divided into 3 groups: the first group consists of fragments of the Life cycle of St. Panteleimon, the second group consists of remnants of the Deesis composition painted over the entrance to the naos with the representations of Jesus Christ, the Mother of God, and St. John the Baptist. The third group consists of fragments of the scenes in the first zone on the north end of the east wall, as well as the fragment of the imperial scene, which can be linked with the donor composition which was painted in the second zone on the north end of the east wall. On the eastern wall of the narthex, next to the door, there is fresco of the Holy Archangel Michael, in lavish cloths. In the higher zone of the Saint Panteleimon churh naos there are frescoes that depict life scenes of the Christ and the Holy Virgin. The most significant frescoes of the Saint Panteleimon Monastery from the 12th century are : *Mourning of Christ, Moving from the Cross, Transfiguration and Purification of the Virgin Mary*. The *Mourning of Christ* composition is particularly impressive for its emotional portrayal of the grief of the Mother of God over the body of her son, whose face expresses pain and deep sorrow. The Holy Mother of God is staring at her dead son s face, whom she is holding in her arms. Her eyebrows are raised and contracted, her lips pressed tightly together and her eyes radiate grief transmitted to the other figures which represent a departure from earlier Byzantine painting where the Nerezi painter paid great attention to expressing the inner feelings of his figures. Frescoes provide harmony in depictions of portraits in regard with movements, and colors, and specific characteristics that occur in depicting people who hand over living as well as realistic scenes with the full expressions and movements. High artistic achievement of fresco-painters is attested in the composition *Moving from the Cross* where mother's pain for lost son is outstandingly depicted. Besides those there are frescoes from the 16th century that were painted after the disastrous earthquake which happened in 1555. The 12th century frescoes inside the little church of Saint Panteleimon in Nerezi village are among the finest in Macedonia.

In the modern buildings of the Saint Panteleimon Monastery courtyard are a hotel and restaurant, with fine views of Skopje and the Vardar valley it is easy to see how the growth of the city has been constrained by the terrain to follow an east-west axis.

Sar planina Mountain Sharr Mountain

The Shar Planina massif /Macedonian side/ is located between the Gostivar and Tetovo valleys in the south-east, the Mavrovo Lake on the south, the Korab Mt massif in the west. From here, with a small part, the Shar Mountain massif enters the Albanian territory, while its northern and north-western parts are located on the territories of Serbia /province of Kosovo and Metohija/ and Montenegro. Sharr Mountain stretches on a surface of 1600 km, 56.25% of its massif is located partially in Macedonia, 43.12% in Serbia and 0.63% in Albania, which makes it one of the largest mountains in the Balkans. Mountain Shara is the largest mountain in Macedonia, 80 km long and around 30 km wide, and its pastures, peaks, valleys, forests, and rivers are immense. Shar planina Mountain is a mountain with glacial relief, beautiful forests, stunning streams and rivers. The Shar Planina Mountain features very interesting vegetation that includes crops grown up to around 1000 meters, forests up to 1700 meters, and above that lie high pastures which encompass around 550 square kilometers. High quality dairy products, mainly cheese and feta cheese, are made in the many sheepfolds on Shar Mountain and the adjacent mountains.

The Shar Mountain has been formed in the Tertiary period. The most upper parts of the Shar mountain had been frozen with large amounts of ice and snow. The Sharr mountain borders extends from the Kosovo's city of Prizren, following the Lepenec River, the city of Kachanik, passes the Serbia/Macedonia border, the canyon of Derven and forms the waste Polog valley. The border passes near the Vardar River spring called Vrutok and goes near the valley of Mavrovo. There the Radika river separates the two highest Macedonian mountains: Shar planina Mountain and Korab Mountain. After that, the border is mounting, reaching the point of junction of three state borders: Macedonian, Serbia-Montenegro and Albanian. The border now follows the road to the Kosovo's small town of Restelica, the river of Globocica, Plavska river, river of Beli Drim and reaches again the city of Prizren. The Shar Mountain has as many as 43 peaks higher than 2500 meters above the sea level ! An interesting fact is that if starting the travel through the Shar planina mountain from the domineering and magnificent Ljuboten peak, it can be accomplished without going down below 2,000 m of altitude all the way to the Korab mountain for at least 80 km!

Twenty seven of the total of 39 mountain glacier lakes of Shar Mountain lie on the Macedonian side of the border. The biggest glacier lake on the mountain is the *Bogovinsko lake,* situated near the Borislaec peak, on the 1960 meters above the sea. It is long 452 m and wide 225 m, with a depth of 2.2 m. Following is the *Crno lake*, situated near the Borislaec peak, on the 2122 meters above the sea. It is long 248 m and wide 185 m, with a depth of 2.2 m. The third biggest glacier lake on the Sharr Mountain is the *Golem gjol lake*, on the 2180 meters above the sea, it is long 290 and wide 115 meters, with a depth of 5,60 m. On the Serbian (Kosovo's) side of the mountain, the most important lakes are: Livadicko (2173 m) near the peak of Livadica, Jazinachko lake (2180 m) near the Ezerska chuka peak, Big lake (2400 m) near the Bistrica peak etc. Around 72 rivers are forming the mountain canyons and valleys on Shar Mountain. The most important rivers on Sharr Mountain are: Vrutochka, Vrapchiska, Golema, Mazdracha, Bogovinska, Kamenjanska, Pena, Leshocka, Belovishka, Vratnichka, Plavska, Sharshtica, Petroshtica, Ljubinska, Restelicka etc. The most important mountain waterfall is is situated on the Belovishka reka (43 meters high). The waterfall of Leshnica (25 m) is situated near the Sharr Mountain peak of Titov vrv, 2747 m.

The most popular winter ski resort in the Macedonia *Popova Shapka* is located on Mount Shara on the Macedonian side on the 1780 meters above sea level, 35 km from the capital Skopje, along very good paved road. Popova Shapka ski resort offers excellent ski environment and hotel accommodations, set far higher than most east European resorts. Visitors not only from Macedonia, but also from many other countries return season after season to Popova Shapka Ski Center to relax, have fun, and experience adventure. Popova Shapka ski resort on Shar Mountain has been a host to both the European and Balkan Ski Championships. There are two ways to get to Popova Shapka ski resort : by car and by rope-railway with a starting location in Tetovo. The rope-railway is 6 km long and it takes about 36 minutes to reach the top. In the past the Popova Šapka Ski Center was extremely popular for skiers of former Yugoslavia, while after a long break, it becomes interesting for nostalgic and the newcomer generations of skiers, intermediate and advanced snowboarders. There are more and more domestic and foreign skiers and visitors to the Popova Sapka Ski Center, which regains its old splendor and reputation. The Popova Sapka Ski Center features a number of ski lifts of the total length of 20 km, while ski lifts are 6070 meters in length, with capacity of 4000 skiers per hour and the average speed of 3 m/hour. The best ski tracks and runaways of the Popova Sapka Ski Center are „Ceripasina",

„Ge", „Sveti Ilija", „Aerodrom", „Mali Jelak" and „Potok" 1 and 2, while the highest peaks of the ski resort are located at the elevation of 2500 meters. The Popova Šapka Ski Center features three ski runs arranged under FIS standards, of which the tracks of Orlova and Jezerino every year hosts the International Sharr Mountain Slalom cup. For the various types of skiers and winter sports skills, and even for the most demanding and advanced skiers can find a suitable ski track in Popova Sapka Ski Center. The great joy is slalom down along the sunny weather from the height of 2500 meters to 1100 meters. The main feature of the Popova Šapka Ski Center is the large number of sunny days during the ski season, as well as the large quantity of snow. Free-ride lovers find here plenty of terrains perfect for ride off the track. The Popova SapkaSki Center specially organizes full-day off-track tours, constructed with the ratrack, with closed cabin, that accommodates 20 skiers.

The Sharplaninec is an ancient livestock guarding breed from the Shar Planina Mt region. It is named after the Shar Planina mountain range where the breed is most common. The Sharplaninec dog was recognized by the United Kennel Club on January 1, 1995. The Sharplaninec has the honor of being recognized by both the Macedonian and the Yugoslav kennel clubs. Thought to be older than the Istrian Shepherd (although not as old a breed as the Greek Shepherd Dog or the Turkish Akbash), this reserved guardian exists in sustainable numbers in Serbia and Montenegro and Macedonia. It was first recognized as a distinct breed in 1930. Since 1975 successful exports have been carried out to the United States and Canada to control coyotes, and this is where its future security rests. It is now gaining recognition as a hard-working, readily able flock guard in the Balkan countries. Numerous in its homeland, the Sharplaninec is still part of the great flock. It is versatile and occasionally works cattle or serves as guard. The highly prized dairy products, mostly the cheese and the feta cheese are produced in numerous dairies on the slopes of the Sharr Mountain and in the surroundings.

Skopje

Skopje is the capital city of Macedonia and its largest urban center and settlement, with about a third of total country population. Skopje is political, cultural, economic and administrative center of Macedonia and without a doubt one of the most peculiar cities of the Balkans. In the ancient time Skopje was known as Scupi which is present day archaeological site at the suburb of the town.

The territory of the present day Skopje has been inhabited since at least 4000 BC and Neolithic remains have been found in the Kale Fortress. In 148 BC the city of *Scupi* became part of the Roman Province of Macedonia when it developed rapidly into large religious center with its own bishop. In the year of 518 the Scupi city was destroyed by a disastrous earthquake. Wonderful architectonic buildings, numerous public baths and the ancient amphitheater built in Roman style, large basilica with mosaic floors of Scupi have completely disappeared. After the division of the Roman Empire in 395 Scupi became part of the Byzantine Empire with the seat in Constantinople. There were the Byzantines and the Bulgarians competed over the rule on Scupi in the early medieval period. Byzantine Emperor Justinian I constructed Kale Fortress in the 6th century. From 1189 Scupi was under the Serbian Medieval Kingdom and its capital city til 1346. In 1392 the city was conquered by the Ottoman Turks who named the town Üsküp. The town stayed under Ottoman control over 500 years. During that period numerous typical Ottoman structures had been built in the oriental architecture such are Bezistan, Stone Bridge, Daut Pasha Hamam and Cifte Hamam, Isa Bey Mosque, Ishak Bey Mosque /Aladja

Mosque/, Kapan Han, Kursumli Han, Suli Han, Sultan Murad Mosque, Mustapha Pasha Mosque, Yahja Pasha Mosque....

In 1912 Skopje was named the capital of the Vardar Banovina of the *Kingdom of Yugoslavia* as per subdivision of the Kingdom of Serbia during the Balkan Wars. After the First World War Skopje became part of the newly formed Kingdom of Serbs, Croats and Slovenes /Kingdom of Yugoslavia/. In the Second World War Skopje was conquered by the Bulgarian Army, which was part of Axis powers. In 1944 Skopje became the capital city of Democratic Macedonia /later Socialist Republic of Macedonia/ which was a federal state and the part of Democratic Federal Yugoslavia /later Socialist Federal Republic of Yugoslavia/. The city of Skopje developed rapidly after the World War II but this trend was interrupted in 1963 when it was hit by a disastrous earthquake, as the town is located in the seismologically extremely active region. This terrible earthquake with a magnitude of 6.1 which hit Skopje caused 1066 dead people when around 80 percent of the city was destroyed, among them many neoclassical and historical buildings in the city centre. In the following years the city of Skopje was largely rebuilt by huge support and donations of all Yugoslav Republics.

In 1991 Skopje became the capital of independent Macedonia. Nowadays it is capital of the North Macedonia, how the country was renamed....

Skopje is set on the upper course of the Vardar River, located approximately in the middle of a major Balkan route that runs north-south between Belgrade and Athens. The Vardar River divides the city in two, the old part and the newer part. The latter has a nice pedestrian street from the Macedonia Square to the old train station. Skopje is the birth place of Mother Teresa, and there is a nice memorial house in her honor and off course a sculpture of her. Skopje lies at an elevation of 225 meters. Skopje features humid subtropical climate with very hot and humid summers and cold, wet, and often snowy winters. Two artificial lakes of Skopje are located just few kilometers outside the city center Matka and Treska Lakes and are supplied by the Treska River. Skopje also has a glacial lake called Jakupica.

Most of the Ottoman monuments of Skopje, many from the 15th and the 16th centuries, are clustered in and around a charming historical core the Old bazaar district /charshi/, which itself is a rare /and living/ example of such an urban ensemble that evolved between the 15th and the 19th centuries. The Old Bazaar of Skopje /Macedonian *Stara Čaršija* from the Turkish, meaning marketplace/ in Skopje represents the old commercial heart of the town and the largest bazaar in the Balkans /besides the one in Istanbul/. The Skopje Old Bazaar is situated on the eastern bank of the Vardar River and had been the city center for trade and commerce since the 12th century.

Ottoman sultan Murat II built a large congregational mosque on the Gazi Baba hill in 1430, perhaps on the foundations of a church that stood derelict since the Ottoman conquest in 1391 or 1392. Ishak Bey, a lord of the march appears to have been the adopted son of no less than the town's conqueror. He sponsored a cluster of buildings on the edge of the emerging commercial district, in the depression below the fortress, including a hospice with a built-in oratory /zaviye/imaret/, a seminary /medrese/, a public bathhouse /hamam/ for both sexes, and a hostel for merchants /han/. It rapidly grew and reached its peak during the Ottoman rule what is evidenced in over 30 mosques, several caravan-serays, hamams /baths/ and other Ottoman structures and monuments. The hans, of which there soon were several, served the traders doing business in the commercial Skopje district. They were housed in cells in two-storied buildings around an enclosed courtyard. The bathhouse Hammam, testimony to a revived bathing culture, was important not only in terms of hygiene but also as a social space, in particular for women. Ishak Bey also built the structure presently known as the Aladža /Alajja 'Colored'/ Mosque /1438-9/ which served to a variety of functions, including the lodging and feeding of guests /often dervishes/, staff, and dependents, as well as communication and ritual. Ishak Bey's intention must have been to develop 'his' Skopje into an urban center which was continued by his son Isa Bey, better known as the founder of *Sarajevo*, another modern Balkan capital.

In the period between the 16th and 17th century, the Old Bazaar of Skopje reached its urban and economic zenith, developing into one of the largest and most significant oriental old bazaars in the Balkans. The Mustafa Pasha mosque /1492/ in Skopje, recently restored, has preserved much of the grandeur of the Ottoman 'classical age'. The domed cube flanked by a three-bay portico and a lofty, slender minaret is the prototype of many mosques built thereafter in the Balkan provinces, especially in Bosnia and Hungary. The portal of the Mustafa Pasha's mosque may rank as one of the finest of its kind in the Balkans. Although Islamic architecture is predominant in the Skopje Old Bazaar, there are several Orthodox Christian churches as well, that are truly worthvisiting. The Old Skopje Bazaar is present day a protected national landmark and contains numerous old craftsmen shops making the "market on a human scale", where visitors are strongly recommended to try *burek* and other tasty breakfast pastries in numerous cafes. The Suli Han is also situated in the Skopje Bazaar and represents a monument of culture. Suli Han Skopje has been considered as one of the most beautiful edifices from the first half of the 15th century whose structure consisted of wide square atrium around which there was a porch with arches from where the rooms were entered in. After the restoration, Suli Han inn in Skopje has more functional usage and it houses the Museum of the Old

Skopje Bazaar and the Academy of fine Arts of Republic of Macedonia.

Srborit was the first Serbian factory for asphalt and tarmac products in the old Skopje, which run its production in Belgrade and Skopje the Mala Stanica by the Balkan Mill. The Mala stanica is situated righ above the former New railway station 1940 today the Museum of Skopje, was turned into the gallery at the address Jordan Mijalkov street, beneath the northern slope of the Vodno Mountain, once the narrow gauge which connected Skopje and Struga. This asphalt factory would have never been established without support and interest of Skopje Municipality, led by the famous architect Josip Mihailovic who was keen to introduce this new activity also in the town on the Vardar river, which greatly enhanced urbanisation of Skopje. About this testify the fact that first streets of Skopje were paved already in June 1932.

On 21 June 2011, the controversial, colossal monument of Alexander the Great, officially called "Warrior on a Horse" was finally erected in Skopje's central square. Close to 30 meters high (including the 10-metre concrete pedestal), the sculpture dominates the capital's central area. The monument, which reportedly weighs 30 tons, is higher than the surrounding buildings. VMRO revives the myth of Alexander the Great, but many Macedonians are still perfectly comfortable with their Slavic roots. All around the huge square and the Stone Bridge there are several monumental buildings that look like enormous palaces being built, surrounded with also very monumental and impressive sculptures representing most significant historical persons of Macedonia Justinian I, Saint Naum, Cyrill and Methodus, Goce Delcev....

Places to see in Skopje : *The Clock Tower /Saat kula/, Daut Pasha's Bath, Kuršumli An, The Aqueduct, The Stone Bridge, Kale Fortress, Mustafa Pasha's Mosque, Saint Savior Church, Saint Panteleimon*

Monastery Gorno Nerezi village, Matka Canyon, gondola to the Millennium Cross on the Vodno Mountain...

Sveti Spas Church /Saint Savior/ Church Skopje

Situated in Skopje's Old Bazaar, the Church of the Holy Savior Crkva Sveti Spas Skopje is characterized by an unusual architectural design and the modest outside appearance. Sveti Spas Church in Skopje is three-nave religious structure, with the arched central nave above which sits the wooden belfry. The courtyard of Sveti Spas Church in Skopje has steps leading down into the tiny church which was built here in the early 19th century on the ruins of an earlier church which had been destroyed in the fire of 1689. Namely, half of the Church of Sveti Spas in Skopje had been constructed underground due to the 17th century edict of the Turkish Sultan that prohibited Christian structures from being higher than mosques. The Sveti Spas Church in Skopje was the only shrine where Serbs were allowed to attend the liturgical services from 1870 til 1918. The Holy Savior Church Skopje contains one of the *most beautiful wooden carved iconostasis in Macedonia,* an early 19th century creation of the famous 'Mijak School of Macedonian wood carvers' *Makarije Frckovski and Petre Filipovic Garkata.* The iconostasis of Sveti Spas Church Skopje is 6 meters high and 10 meters long. On this wonderfully carved iconostasis, the carving group had managed to show numerous scenes from the Bible, important geometrical ornaments and figures from the flora and the fauna, as well as a little self portrait while working. Part of the fresco painting on the southern side was found from this older church which dates from the 16th century. The founder of the Macedonian Liberation movement of 1903 and its most prominent member, *Goce Delcev,* is buried in the courtyard of the Sveti Spas Church in Skopje that is since 1945 the mausoleum of this revolutionary.

Mustapha Pasha Mosque Skopje

Mustafa Pasha Mosque stands on a plateau above the Old Skopje bazaar, and is the most beautiful Islamic building in Macedonia. It was built in 1492 by Mustafa Pasha, vesir on the court of Sultan Selim I. The Mustafa Pasha mosque is quite elegant and intact, and no additions have been made through the years. The interior is beautiful, simple and spacious. Take few steps back to observe the game of the domes of the fountain, the porch and the mosque. In the turbe next to the mosque the daughter of Mustafa Pasha is buried. The Mustapha Pasha Mosque Skopje has a pleasant rose garden and it offers fine views over the bazaar.

Millennium Cross Skopje

The Millennium Cross is a 66 meters-high cross situated on the top of the Vodno Mountain in Skopje, Republic of Macedonia. The cross was constructed to commemorate 2,000 years of Christianity in Macedonia and the world. The construction of the Millennium Cross began in 2002 and was funded by the Macedonian Orthodox Church, the Macedonian government and donations from Macedonians from all over the world. The cross was built on the highest point of the Vodno Mountain on a place known since the time of the Ottoman Empire as "Krstovar", meaning "Place of the cross", as there was a smaller cross situated there. On 8 September 2008, the independence day of the Republic of Macedonia, an elevator was installed inside the cross. Restaurant and a souvenir shop are next to the cross.

Scupi Archaeological Site

The archaeological site of the ancient Scupi Antique Roman city of Skupi Colonia Flavia Scupinorum is located 3 km north of Skopje, near the villages of Bardovci and Zlokukani. The beginnings of this city are linked with the incursions of the Roman legions in the late 1st century BC and the founding of the Roman province of Moesia in 15 AD. First mentioned in the year 3 BC, it quickly developed into an important regional center when the Romans made it the capital of their Province, with important administrative, economic, cultural, religious and transit facilities of the province Moesia Superior. Scupi began as a Roman legionary camp and the starting point for conquering Dardania and Moesia (possibly housing the 5th Macedonian and/or 4th Scythian legions /Legio V Macedonica and Legio quarta Scythica/ with the soldiers building a considerable settlement for themselves on the site of an older settlement. The Romans located Scupi along important roads that connected the Aegean Sea with central Europe, Thrace with the Adriatic coast. During the Flavian dynasty in 84/5 it acquired the status of a self-governing deductive colony (Colonia Flavia Scupinorum) with the settling of veterans, mainly those from Legio VII Claudia. In the late 3rd century it became the metropolis of the newly established province of Dardania, and in the 4th century it experienced once again great economic and urban growth. Most likely Roman army veterans began to settle there, while the army was still based at Scupi, but once it left northward to take up base at the Danube, local inhabitants (possibly from the nearby ancient town of Stobi) joined them, moving into the abandoned army base. With the creation of a Christian Episcopacy a few centuries later, the economical and cultural importance of Scupi grew yet again. Although it suffered under the Gothic ravages of the 3rd and the 4th century once again the city of Scupi prospered and served briefly as the headquarters of emperor Theodosius. A disastrous earthquake in 518 AD destroyed the city of Scupi. Wonderful architectonic buildings, numerous public baths and the ancient amphitheater built in Roman style, large basilica with mosaic floors of Scupi have completely disappeared. After the division of the Roman Empire in 395 Scupi became part of the Byzantine Empire with the seat in Constantinople. There were the Byzantines and the

Bulgarians competed over the rule on Scupi in the early medieval period.

Nowadays Skupi is one of the largest Roman cities in the Balkans with the status of a colony. Approximately 1,000 graves from the southeast and northwest necropolises have been explored, which date from the period between the 1st and the 4th centuries, as well as parts of the Antique bridge across the river Vardar, a private villa and a Christian basilica in the village of Bardovci.

Stobi Archaeological Site

The ancient city of Stobi lies in a fertile valley of central Macedonia, 15 km away from town of Kavadarci, about 80 km south of *Skopje* and about 85 km from the Macedonian-Greek border. The Stobi site is just few minutes off the central north-south highway that connects Macedonia with Greece, on the place where the Crna Reka River (Erigon) joins the Vardar River (Axious). Stobi was established on the crossing point of the major *vital trade routes* that led from the Danube to the Aegean Sea the road that connected *Via Egnatia and Via Militaris /Via Axis/* and *Via Diagonalis*, that traversed Macedonia in its days, making it important strategically as a center for both trade and warfare.

This crossroad of ancient civilizations has left a rich historical and *cultural legacy of the Stobi* antique theaters, palace ruins, basilicas, brightly-colored mosaics, famous tetra-conchal baptistery and religious relics for visitors to enjoy today. Archaeological explorations in Stobi began in World War I. As a city, Stobi is first mentioned in documents from the 2nd century BC by Titus Livius, the Roman historian, who records the military victory of the Macedonian king Philip V over the Dardanian invaders "near Stobi" in 197 BC. However, archaeologists believe that the town of Stobi had been inhabited from at least 400 years earlier, as archaeological finds testify to the fact that the site was settled continually since prehistoric times. From the 3rd-4th century AD Stobi became a rich and prosperous city, but also an important Christian center due to its location on the crossroads of important trade routes, when the city had experienced its biggest period of growth. Stobi was the biggest Roman city in Macedonia and later became the capital of the province of Macedonia Secunda, the urban, military, administrative, trading, and religious center of that region for the Roman and the early Byzantine empires. The episcopal basilica of the bishop Philip, from the 5th century, shows just how influential this city was as a religious center. The most important Christian building in Stobi was constructed, its interior was majestic, with white marble and mosaic floors. South of the basilica is a baptistery, with an inscribed quadrennial at its center, which was covered by a dome for a time. The floor is decorated with mosaics of peacocks and deer. In 447 AD Stobi was destroyed by the Huns as many other towns on the Balkans. On their way to Dyrrachium, Theodoric and the Ostrogoths robbed Stobi but this was not as disastrous as the attack of the Huns. The beginning of the 6th century is marked by the huge earthquake in 518 AD which ruined many towns in Dardania and Macedonia Secunda.

The Stobi archaeological site /located just 3 km from the Gradsko exit on Highway E-75/ is must see as it offers spectacular insight into the antiquity and sweeping views of the central Macedonian plain, and makes very popular tourist destination in Macedonia. Ancient Site of Stobi contains numerous structures and buildings such as the 2nd century impressive amphitheater, Episcopal Basilica and Residence, the Theodosian Palace, streets, baths, textile workshop, large houses with interior peristyle courts decorated with resplendent fountains and mosaic floors, villas and early Christian ruins with extensive and ornate mosaic floors. Excavations and conservation works of the Stobi site are constantly carried out.

Struga

Struga is situated on the northern shore of Ohrid Lake on the banks of Black Drim River, at the foothill of the *Jablanica Mountain*, 12 km from Kafasan border crossing that leads to the neighboring Albania. The Jablanica Mountain is known as a place where the famous Roman caravan road Via Egnatia once was passing. The Black Drim River divides the city of Struga into two banks that are interconnected with 7 bridges. The river represents the end of the lake and the beginning of the river Drim basin, shaping the two artificial lakes of Globocica and Debar lake whose water is used to produce electricity in two hydroelectric plants.

Struga is an ancient Balkan settlement with traces of living since the Neolithic times. In the antique period it was called Enchalon an eel. Struga is founded on the spot where the greenish Black Drim River flows out of Ohrid Lake which is the starting point of eel's long journey that leads to the Sargasso Sea where eel fulfills its biological needs for continuation of the species. Town of Struga features a picturesque beauty, wonderful sighs and many of old monuments, like the clay chamberpots at the House of the Miladinov Brothers, the famous old Struga bazaar, the century old churches and mosques. The architecture of Struga is characterized by the wonderful richly decorated houses of the wealthy citizens. Struga is also a place of important cultural significance in the Republic of Macedonia, as it is the birthplace of the poets Konstantin and Dimitar Miladinov. Struga's location on the Lake of Ohrid makes it a slightly quieter and more peaceful experience than the more bustling tourist center of Ohrid. The Sveta Bogorodica Church The Holy Virgin church in the village of Vraništa is believed to be the one where Tsar Samuel was crowned.

Since the year of 1961, Struga is a host of the internationally famous festival of poetry known as "Struga Poetry Evenings"

Struskite veceri poezije. The Struga Poetry festival is held every year towards the end of August and is the world's largest event of this kind. Struga Festival laureates include several Nobel Prize for Literature winners such as Joseph Brodsky, Eugenio Montale, Pablo Neruda, Seamus Heaney, Fazıl Hüsnü Dağlarca and many others. The Struga Poetry Evenings and "the traveling of the eel" are the two main world attractions that Struga's inhabitants are proud of.

Places to see : Black Drim River, Early-Christian Basilica in Oktisi village, Archangel Michael Cave Church in Radozda village, Nativity of the Holy Virgin Cave Church in Kalista village. There is a possibility of buying the famous monastery cheese and locally-produced grapes brandy (rakija).

Trebeništa Trebenishte

At the end of the First Worl War, the Bulgarians discovered in occupied South Serbia on Ohrid Lake shore the Archaic necropolis and took and transferred all excavated artifacts and items to the National Museum in Sofia. The discovery of the rich treasures in Trebenista village in 1918, located on the road from Ohrid to Kicevo, was like something out of a movie : ancient aristocratic graves loaded with gold and silver items, beautifully adorned burial funeral masks and gifts fit for a king....

The site of Trebenista with necropolis, dating from the 7th 4th centuries BC was discovered accidentally by Bulgarian soldiers in the field called Grobac, beneath the Gornic hamlet. Trebeniste Necropolis is regarded as one of the most interesting archaeological sites from the Iron age on the Balkan Peninsula. It is believed that the necropolis was used by the people from the ancient town of Lychnidos. In the past, the Trebeniste region was renowned for its rich silver bed the Damastius silver mines mentioned by Strabo were nearby. The most important Balkan roads used to intersect there as well, as the important Via Egnatia road stretching in all four directions of the world. Three and a half kilometers west of Lake Ohrid lies a plain crossed by the Drin river. The mountains of present day Albania separate this area from the Adriatic Sea. Two rivers, Shkumbin (Genesis) and Semeni (Aspus), connect this land to the shore.

Fifty six tombs were discovered of which most significant and the oldest are the 12 princely tombs, a whole dynasty that was buried with all the marks of their power, or tombs of warriors of high social status. Four wonderfully crafted golden burial masks, approximately in the size of a human face, golden hand with a ring, sandals, golden gloves, gold, silver, and bronze vessels and jewelry and rosettes have been discovered on three male and one female skeleton in Trebenista village. Trebeniste site finds are housed in the Archaeological Museums in Ohrid, Sofia and Belgrade. A very similar funeral mask was discovered in 2002, by Pasko Kuzman, in the Samoil Fortress in Ohrid. Trebeniste necropolis remains today one of the most important archaeological finds in Macedonia, and a vivid reminder of the style and sophistication of past cultures.
Nikola Vulic

Treskavec Monastery

Treskavec Monastery is situated at the altitude of 1300 meters, about 10 km away from town of Prilep, under the Zlatovrv peak 1422 meters, in a striking remote mountain landscape of karst massif, from where you have a stunning view of the Pelagonia Valley and towns of Prilep, Bitola and Kruševo. It is said that Treskavec Monastery is one of the most inaccessible and hidden monasteries in Macedonia, since it can be reached only on foot, along the winding narrow pathway passing by strange rock formations. We find Treskavac Monastery one of the most beautiful monasteries in the Balkans and a significant monastic and spiritual center of Ohrid Archbishopric. From Treskavac Monastery visitors can observe the most stunning sunset in Macedonia, dominating the beautiful Pelagonija Plain.

The complex of Treskavec Monastery consists of the single-nave church with a central dome and the three-sided eastern altar apse, dedicated to "Assumption of the Holy Mother", monastery dormitory and the dining room. It is thought that the Treskavec Monastery was built in the 13th century on the remnants of the early-Christian temple, according to the written inscription at the entrance, and had been renovated and richly donated in the 14th century by the King Milutin. King Dušan became donor of the Treskavac Monastery after his victory against the Byzantine Empire in 1334. Treskavac Monastery was built during the Ottoman rule over this region in the architectural traditions developed under the influence of the Byzantine school. Treskavac Monastery's façade is made from faded red bricks, with ornamental external niches and uneven roof. The Treskavac Church was fresco-painted in the 14th and the 15th century. Frescoes dating from the 14th century in the exo-narthex of the Assumption of the Holy Mother Church of Treskavac Monastery were completed in three periods : the oldest frescoes, whose donor was King Dušan, date from 1334-1343, depicting the church calendar, while frescoes of the former facade of the later added chapel, that represent founder's composition and those painted on the facade of the exo narthex, date from the middle of the 15th century. Greek masters, used to accomplish themes and tendencies of the imperial paintings have created new manners, contrary to the ancient comparisons about similarities between the celestial and the terrestrial courts.

The Christ as the Emperor of all Emperors *rex regnanticum* dressed in the modern costume of Basileus is depicted in the north-eastern calotte. The nine angelic choirs in court dresses are painted around the central medallion, in the circle, while the crowned Virgin stands before the empty throne. Owing to the cult of the Mother of God of Treskavac, the Treskavec Monastery has been since the Medieval times a pilgrimage center visited by faithful people, and members of the royal family as well, such as the young King Uroš, son of Emperor Dušan. The neighboring small cave church which has been recently registered in the immediate vicinity of the Treskavac Monastery and the remains of a hermitage imply some forms of eremite life. Treskavac Monastery experienced most prosperous period during the reign of King Dusan when it possessed large estate and 20 surrounding villages.

Veles

Veles is a Macedonian city on both sides of the Vardar River, located in the Povardarie region of North Macedonia, on the main crossroads of the Balkans leading from north to the Aegean Sea, in the large and fertile valleys of the Morava and Vardar rivers. In medieval times the city of Veles was a big and rich trading center and manufacturer of silk, lead and porcelain. Two railways go through Veles one direction East of Macedonia to Stip and Kocani, and another to the southwestern part to Bitola. To the northwest of Veles is Skopje the capital of Macedonia, the city of Sveti Nikole is to the northeast, the city of Stip is to the east, Prilep is to the southwest and Kavadarci and Negotino are in the southeast.

Veles is very old historical settlement, known as the *cradle of Macedonian culture* which features rather unique cityscape of red roofs houses that that represent the important trading role the town played from the earliest history. The settlement is first time recorded in the 3rd century as *Bila Zora or Vila Zora. Even today there is the Mountain of Bela Zora in vicinity of Veles. Veles was center of a number of Christian Orthodox churches built by the*

Medieval Serbian royalty and rulers. Here was the Church of Saint Archangel built before 1348, and the Church of Saint Demetrius recorded in 1300, while the Monastery of Saint John near Veles was erected during the Turkish reign in 1670, as since 1395 and the Ottoman conquest it was named 'Kjupurli' "city of bridges".

The present name of Veles dates from the 7th century AD after the Slavic word of *les* which means forest, due to lush forests that always surrounded this settlement. God Veles is deity of cattle, crops, wisdom, arts, richness, ownership, magic, fraud, trade, prediction, virtues and leader of souls of the dead. The God of Veles is protector of shepherds and magicians (volhvov or volhov). Volhovs were Slavic wizards. The origin of their name includes the Volos, who surely was protector of magicians and wizards. The reason that Slavic population venerated God of Veles is their belief in this deity on whom their survival depended. God Veles was involved for crops, fields and both domestic and wild animals. Whatever was the form of society cattle-raising or hunters or agriculture it was dependent on the God Veles. Also tha magic and wisdom played important role in local lives of Slavs. Magic is connected even today with music and a number of religions, so the God Veles is also protector or music which was always considered somehow magical and language of gods. Musicians were talented people, capable to transmit the divine inspiration and create magical melodies. Veles as god is also represented in another form as a bear, that in Slavic mythology represents the forest ruler who cares about animals, forest products and the forest itself.

In the 12th and the 13th century the settlement of Veles was important episcopal seat with well-developed trade, crafts and pottery. In 1689 Veles experienced large destruction when it was occupied by the Austrian army as were Skopje and Stip, under leadership of General Eney Picolomini who had burned and plundered those cities during army retreat towards north, escaping from the fierce and vindictive Turkish campaign. After the Balkan wars and the First WW, Veles lost its power when the number of population stagnates and declined. In communist times Veles was called by the name Titov Veles, in honor of the Marshal Josip Broz Tito, when it was big industrial, administrative and economic hub of Yugoslavia in the heart of the Republic of Macedonia, which successfully processed and exported lead and zink and porcelain, with thousands of employees in numerous big factories.

The terrain configuration of the town of Veles on both sides of the Vardar River greatly contributed to the specific urban architectural style of houses for which construction was used the rough stone as the excellent foundations. Houses of Veles usually have two or three floors, rarely more floors. The upper floors of Veles houses feature belvedere /porch/ with numerous windows, mostly of white washed facades. The main characteristic of the Veles architecture are girders that enable extension of the upper floors of houses that look fully highlighted. Houses of Veles are located in rows one above the other , and the most significant houses stand out themselves from the neighboring ones the Houses of Pauns, Trenche, Prnarovs, Djorgovs, Sukarevs....

The *Veles Clock Tower* is symbol of the town dating from the 16th century. Originally it used as the observation point across the Vardar River, but in the 18th century during the revival of Veles, it was turned into the town clock. The old Clock Tower of Veles was built of polished stone, and features a lavish upper part, ringing only 3 minutes prior and after a full hour. The Veles Clock Tower provides wonderful panorama of the town and its surrounding, surely making one of the tourist attractions of Veles. The central monument of Veles comes as the impressive horse rider and is dedicated to prominent Ilinden heroes who took part in the Ilinden Uprising for liberation of Macedonia Jovan Naumov Alabaka, Andrej Dimov Dorucev, Todor Hristov and other local heroes....

The *Veles city cathedral church of Saint Panteleimon* is located in a cavern southwest of Veles, several hundred meters from the last houses. The Saint Panteleimon church is under the protection of UNESCO and is the Cathedral of the Vardar Orthodox diocese. The frescoes and icons of Saint Panteleimon Church are the artwork of famous Macedonian painters from the Mijak area, Papradishte and Veles region. Most icons of Saint Panteleimon church were painted by the talented painters Gjorgji Damjanov and Gjorgji Jakov Zografski. The prominent Balkan architect of the late-Ottoman era, Andreja Damjanov or Damjanovic is buried in the Saint Panteleimon churchyard, in the church he designed. Architect Andreja Damjanovic designed many churches and monasteries in the Balkans the Holy Virgin church in Skopje in 1835, the Saint John in Kratovo, 1836, Saint Panteleimon in Veles in 1840, Saint Nicholas in Novo Selo near Stip in 1850, Saint Nicholas church in Kumanovo in 1851, Saint George church in Smederevo in 1854, Saint Trinity Church in Mostar in 1873, the Birth of the Holy Virgin church in Sarajevo 1868, as well as the church within the Saint Joachim Monastery Osogovo complex in 1851, the churches in Pecenjevce and Turakovac villages….

The Spomenik Kosturnica (Memorial Ossuary) in Veles was built to commemorate the Partisan soldiers who fought for the freedom of Veles and Macedonia during the National Liberation War from 1941 to 1945 against the fascist German and Bulgarian forces. This monument also serves as a resting place in the form of an underground crypt for the remains of roughly one hundred fallen Partisan soldiers from the Veles area.

Monastery of Saint Demetrius (Манастир Св. Димитрија), situated few kilometers south of Veles was built in the 14th century by King Stefan Dušan. The Byzantine-style church has a bell tower built into its western side. The unique feature of this Monastery is the fresco depicting the Doomsday on the northern wall of the narthex. This fresco composition depicts a large fish eating a person sinner, and more sea monsters, as well as three persons next to them, of which one is reading. Church of Saint John the Baptist (Црква „Св. Јован Крстител") is the oldest church in Veles, most likely constructed in the 13th century. It is a small church built of stone, situated some 100 meters north of the Monastery of Saint Demetrius.

Monument and grave of duke Jovan Stojkovic Babunski /Serbian Chetnik commander in Macedonian struggle and the last great hero of Stara Srbija-Old Serbia/ was demolished by Bulgarian during their occupation, when bones of this hero were thrown in the Vardar River. He was born in the village of Martolci near Veles and is remembered as great fighter and protector of the Serb population terrorized by the Turks and Arnauts. Jovan Stojkovic Babunski bravely fought in the firts rows in the Battle of Kumanovo in 1912 and the Salonica Break in 1918, and until his death in 1920 he tirelessly destroyed enemies of Serbia.

In the village of Tomislavljevo today Donje and Gornje Karaslari village, in the Vardar River valley, 11 km southeast of Veles, the Memorial Ossuary was erected with remains of 1500 Serbian soldiers of the Veles area killed in the wars 1912-1918 and who died from cholera in 1913. Initiative for collecting scattered graves into a common Memorial and construction of the chapel above it dedicated to the Holy King Stefan Decanski came from arch-priest Nikola Jovicevic from Veles, as per data from 1925 about a large graveyard which was left deserted and nearly forgotten. Committee for transmission of soldiers remains, led by the priest Nikola, was created from reputed locals of this area, Christians and Muslims, with great contribution of the army and local Turks of the Tomislavljevo village the Karaslari village. Since there were remains of the French soldiers in the graves all around the village, they were buried in a separate ossuary. King Aleksandar Karađorđević donated a bell for the Memorial chapel which was 308 kg in weight, and since 1941 was removed from this place. By the efforts of professor Bora Ristić from Skopje, the Memorial Chapel in the village of Karaslari was reconstructed to keep eternal memory of the heroic brothers by arms!

Veljuša Monastery

Built on a rocky plateau, Veljuša Monastery or the monastery of The Holy Mother of God Eleusa is located in the village of Veljuša, about 7 kilometers west of Strumica. There is the beautiful view of the Strumica Valley from the Monastery. The Veljuša Monastery was founded in 1080 by the monk Manuel, who spent most of his ascetic life in Asia Minor and upon arrival to Veljusa village later became Bishop of Strumica. There are numerous written sources about this monastery, most of which are kept in the archives of the Iviron Monastery on Mount Athos. Out of the many written documents, the two most prevalent are the marble plaques on the lintel of the entrance door of the monastery. These marble plaques are of recent date due to the fact that during World War I the original ones were taken to the Archaeological Museum in Sofia. The other important documents are the charter of the Byzantine emperor Alexius I Comnenus dating from the July 1085, by which the Veljuša Monastery was granted autonomy and the status of a royal monastery and the Rule (typikon) of Manuel I Comnenus of 1152 which has also survived. The later documents on the land property granted to the Veljuša Monastery contains an inventory of monastery possessions dating from 1164, where all valuables of the monastery were listed. However, in the 13th century the Veljuša Monastery lost its autonomy and until 1913 was under the authority of the Iviron Monastery on Mount Athos. In 1913, having decided to abandon the Veljuša Monastery, the monks set it on fire which resulted in damaged fresco painting to a great extent.

However, the monastery's original architecture has been well preserved and it represents a rare structure of the 11th Century in Macedonia.

Veljuša Monastery is a four-apse structure with three domes, embellished with ceramic and poly-chrome decorations. The exo-narthex of the southern porch of the Veljuša Monastery shows the Cross of Veljusa as well as the figure of St. Onophrius in the desert when visited by the monk St. Panfnutius. The exo-narthex displays the figure of Manuel holding the Veljusa monastery in his hand. The fresco painting had been done in three phases: the first one in 1081, the second one in 1164, and the third one, considered non canonical, in the 19th century. The fresco in the dome represents Christ the Pantocrator ("Almighty" or "All-powerful") and the fresco in the nave portrays the Holy Mother of God "Theotokos Oranta"- flanked by St. John the Baptist, two archangels and four prophets. The altar space of the Veljusa Monastery shows the fresco of the Holy Mother of God Theotokos Nikopoia and Christ enthroned are depicted in the altar space as well as the liturgical service of the holy hierarchs with the Hetimazia (the Sacrifice of Jesus). The north apse shows the Descent of Christ into Hell, the east one the Holy Mother of God with Christ, the south one the Annunciation, and the west one The Meeting of our Lord. The southern chapel, which is dedicated to St. Savior, shows Jesus Christ Emanuel as a twelve-year-old child. The eastern wall shows Jesus in Glory together with a portrait of St. Nyphon; the western shows St. Panteleimon. The Veljuša church's naos contains a reconstructed altar partition from marble, and the floor is decorated with mosaics that form geometrical shapes. Today, the Veljuša monastery houses the monastic dormitory of Strumica sisterhood. There are auxiliary buildings on the premises including a clock tower /added in the 20th century/, a bakery, an inn, and a small chapel dedicated to the Apostle and Saint Paul and to Saint Gregory Palamas.

At the time of construction of the Veljuša church, the village was called Paleokastro, but later it got its present name after the monastery of Veljusa (derived from Eleusa). The rich historical documents originally preserved in this monastery (available in Monastery of Iviron on Mountain Athos), Church of St. Mary Merciful (Eleusa) takes the most significant place in the ecclesiastical and cultural history, not only in the south-eastern part of Macedonia but also in the Balkans.

Vevčani Village Vevcani Springs

The village of Vevcni or Vevčani village is located at a distance of 14 km from Struga town and Ohrid lake, at the foot of the gorgeous Jablanica mountain range. It is assumed by the researchers that the village of Vevčani was founded sometime from the end of the 6th century to the beginning of the 8th century. The Vevcani village was founded most probably by Berziti people, who had adopted Christianity at that time. The first settlement of Vevcani was originally set at the foot of the Jablanica mountain. The villages of Labuništa, Podgorci, Krstec, Jablanica and Vevčani in Drimkol area were the Serb-patriarchal villages with predominant Serb population of Old Serbia. Drimkol refers to the ethnic-geographic area in western part of North Macedonia, on the border with Albania. The name of Drimkol is of Turkish origin and was created from the name of the Drim River and the Turkish expression of *kol* which means small county or area. Drimkol area borders with the Crni Drim River on the west, with the Jablanica Mountain in the east, with the Ohrid Lake to the south and to the north with the Debar zhupa county. Drimkol is divided into the Debar Drimkol in the north and the Struga Drimkol which enters the Stuga valley.

The Vevcani village is home to well-preserved authentic architecture, 19 Churches, Monasteries and Chapels, eco environment. The central church of the Vevcani village however is dedicated to Saint Nicholas and dates back from 1876. A prominent Vevcani monastery is Sveti Spas which is situated at over 1300 meters above sea level, right above the Vevcani village. In the vicinity and within wonderful surroundings of the Vevčani village there are many wonderful glacial lakes and abundance of fresh waters. The highest and most prominent Vevcani glacial lake is "Lokva" which is situated at over 2000 meters above sea level on Jablanica Mountain. The famous Vevčani springs are some of the most famous springs to be found in Macedonia and the Balkans, but surely the most beautiful natural attraction of Macedonia. The Vevcani springs are located on the eastern slope of the Jablanica mountain range whose fragrant slopes run through the village of Vevčani at an approximately sea level altitude at over 900 meters. The largest Vevcani spring is located at the opening of one of the many caves in the region. Below the largest Vevcani spring are ten minor springs which all converge together. The most famous Vevcani spring is "Jankov Kamen" which is situated at 1200 meters above sea level. Another spring is "Mala Livada" from which the water has a unique flavor and color. It is situated at over 1600 meters above sea level. The highest Vevcani spring is "Golina" situated at over 2000 meters above sea level. The rate of water flow from the Vevcani springs is estimated to exceed the rate of 1500 liters per second, most notably in Spring. The hydro-logical site Vevchanski Izvori (Vevchani Springs) was proclaimed Natural Monument in 1999.

The total number of inhabitants in picturesque Vevčani village is around 2500. The Vevčani village has a local self government of its own. Vevcani village or Village of Vevcani, and Struga are easily accessible by bus, car and other modes of transport. The tourists can stay either in the hotels of Struga or in the authentic and nicely appointed private houses/pensions or highly comfortable boarding houses in Vevcani village that can accommodate mainly smaller tourists groups.

Thousands of tourists flock to the Vevcani village during the exciting Vevcani village Carnival that is organized on the 13th and 14th January celebrated as Saint Basil's Day. The Vevcani Carnival dates back to the pagan times, that is almost 1300 years old. During the Vevcani Carnival different colorful events of the recent times are acted out by the villagers with a masks on their face, imitating devils, demons and other mythical characters while performing peculiar movements, gesticulations, and screams. Traditional music is played on zurlas /a traditional double-reed wood wind instrument/ and drums.

There are 8 traditional restaurants and boarding houses in Village Vevčani, Struga that provide relaxation, refreshment and delicious experiences to tourists. Pupina Kuka /the Birth-house of Mihajlo Pupin/ and Domakinska kuka and Kutmičevica and Via Egnatia Restaurants are popular Vevcani local restaurants serving traditional specialties and great Macedonian delights. In those restaurants visitors can experience the true lifestyle and customs in various workshops live music, folklore music performances of the highly talented and skilled local folklore club of Drimkol, self-cooking classes of preparation of traditional food with active participation of guests... The Vevčani village has its own official coat-of-arms and symbol which is a Magic cauldron with two clowns dancing over it. The Vevčani passport is also available here.

Vodoca Monastery

The Vodoča Monastery with its Byzantine style church dedicated to Saint Leontius /Holy Martyr Leontius/ is situated at the exit from Vodoča village, only 4 km northwest of Strumica in southeast Macedonia. Vodoča Monastery was mentioned for the first time in

1018 in the charters of the Byzantine Emperor Basil the Second, at the time when Tzar Samuel's state the First Bulgarian Kingdon was destroyed. This shrine appears again in the historical archives of the Chilandary Monastery act from 1376, when the Vodoča Bishop Daniel and the Bansko Bishop Gregory settled their disputes with the local secular authorities over the borders of the Chilandary Monastery estates in the Strumica area. The oral tradition has it that this monastery was the first gathering place and the first religious place of the first Christians in the Strumica area.

The present outward appearance of Vodoča Monastery the Saint Leontius church depicts the former splendor. Still, the interior setting, containing the multitude frescoes, the marble iconostasis, the large-scale throne icons, the opulent sacred vessels, the procession banners and precious adornments, the furniture and the liturgical utensils... have been lost for ever. There are no exact historical records on the construction of the Vodoča church. In fact, it is a complex of Vodoča churches with three construction phases. The oldest church is situated in the eastern side of the present day church containing only a small fragment of that remained in the altar space. The second phase is when the original Vodoča basilica was ruined and in the first half of the 11th century to the west side a church was built in the form of an inscribed cross, dedicated to the Entry into the Temple of the Most Holy Virgin. The only frescoes preserved until today are those of St. Euplus and St. Isaurius dating from that period, indicating analogies with the fresco painting in the Ohrid Holy Sophia Basilica and with the one in the Holy Healers' church in Kostur /Greece/. In the 12th century an extension of the Vodoča Church was carried out, during which the large eastern cruciform church was built, which has monumental fresco painting. To the west part of the Vodoča church, in the second half of the 14th century, the narthex was built, fresco painted in that century.

When the uncovered porch in the southern part was built, it is not known.

The Vodoca Monastery is far famous after a dreadful event and as a place where 14000 soldiers of Tzar Samuil were blinded, after their defeat in the Battle on Belasica Mountain by the Byzantine Emperor Basil the Second, after which the village was named. Vodoča Monastery is silent testimony to the magnificence of the ancient seat of Strumica metropolitan. At night this sight is yet more majestic. The whole Vodoča Monastery complex is lightened from various angles. Amid the surrounding darkness the chance traveler gets the feeling as if the monastery were pending, in descent from the heavens.

Zrze Monastery Zrze village

The Zrze monastery complex is located at an elevation of 1000 meters, near and actually above the Zrze village, approximately 30 km north-west of Prilep, on slopes of the gorgeous Dautica Mountain, dominating the Pelagonija Plain in Central-western Macedonia. The Zrze Monastery complex, called and known as the Zrze Monastery consists of several Medieval churches under the same roof the Holy Transfiguration Church, Saint Peter and Paul Church, the Chapel of St. George and St. Nicholas, that with remnants of an early Christian basilica from the 5th or the 6th century, testify of the rich cultural tradition of the Prilep area. There are the numerous monk cells beneath the Zrze monastic complex, and their large number indicates the monastic complex as the substantial religious center and the rich spiritual life of the monks, who belonged to the highest monastical order.

The main church of the Transfiguration of the Zrze monastic complex is a single nave building, with a semicircular apse on the eastern side. Zrze Monastery was built by monk German in the mid-

14th century, during the reign of Serbian King Dusan. Before 1368/1369 the western porch was added. At that time the Orthodox Metropolitan seat was in Prilep with the Archbishop Jovan as appointed Metropolitan. Archbishop Jovan and his brother Makarios were distinguished monks-painters who devoted their lives to fresco-decoration of the Medieval Orthodox monasteries and found their final rest in Zrze Monastery. They both, accompanied with the monk Gregory took care about the Zrze Monastery and in the 14th century painted it with frescoes. Their frescoes are preserved in fragments and feature precious drawing and skillful composition with the old style of modulation harmonized and distant coloring that is related to the possible Byzantine experienced teachers of painting of the traditional discourse. Monumental feature of those Zrze frescoes is not persuasive. Intentions of painters were clear to express the broadness and festivity of the old style by large forms and epic clear compositions, often borrowed from the 13th century. However meticulousness attributed to the new era took away the inner strengths from the painting. The fresco of the Holy Virgin with Christ depicted in niche above the entrance to the Transfiguration church is surely the unsigned work of Makarios. Two large precious and highly venerated icons of Zrze Monastery distinguish themselves from the others by their beauty and status of preservation : the Christ-Life giver painted by Archbishop Jovan in 1394 and The Holy Virgin Pelagonitsa with Christ, a which is work of his brother Makarios from 1422.

Brothers painters /zographs/ Archbishop Jovan and his brother Makarios painted also numerous monasteries of the time built in the region. When Turks occupied the Balkans, brothers ceded the maintenance of the Zrze Monastery to the mayor Konstantin and sons. Zrze Monastery was abandoned during the reign of Ottoman Sultan Bayazed I to be seriously damaged at the beginning of the

16th century. It was reconstructed in 1535 and in the 17th century its construction was completed by adding a porch and extension. The church of St. Peter and Paul had been built on the northern side of the Zrze monastic complex, later known as the Shepherds' church. According to a legend, both Kings Vukasin and his son, Prince Marko, got married in the Zrze Monastery.

Today, Zrze Monastery complex consists of the several churches and chapels, the dormitory and some accessory rooms. The Zrze Monastery itself and the village below it, feature archaic and authentic architecture : houses with balconies decorated with flowers, wrapped up with peacefulness and deep tranquility and spirituality.

The End

Made in the USA
Las Vegas, NV
29 March 2025